Cinderella & Rockerfella

A panto-style musical by Mark and Helen Johnson
Script by Sue Langwade

The Songs

Act One
- Song 1 — Tonight's The Night
- Song 2 — A Friend Like You
- Song 3 — It's Not All It's Cracked Up To Be
- Song 4 — I'm So In Love With Me!
- Song 5 — You're Going To The Ball

Act Two
- Song 6 — There's A Party Here Tonight
- Song 7 — A Ton Of Love
- Song 8 — If I Had One Wish
- Song 9 — Your Feet Are Too Big!
- Song 10 — Happy Ever Afters

© 2008 Out of the Ark Ltd, Middlesex TW12 2HD

A BRIEF HISTORY OF
PANTOMIME

The traditional British pantomime as we know and love it today has its roots in several earlier traditions, from medieval morality plays to Victorian musical hall, with a few other stops along the way! Below are some of the elements which are now considered essential for a show to be true 'pantomime' and we've also included a few interesting facts! If you would like to find out more about the fascinating history of this unique art form, visit www.its-behind-you.com.

Audience Participation — This is a must, usually including a singalong, an 'It's behind you' routine and some 'Oh no I'm not'/'Oh yes you are!' interaction.

Goodies and Baddies — Traditionally baddies enter from stage left* and goodies stage right* – this dates back to the heaven/hell entrances of the medieval morality plays, which were always arranged this way.

Boys or Girls? — Until quite recently the Principal Boy (the hero of the piece) was traditionally played by a female and the female 'Dame' character/s is/are still usually played by a male. This is thought to date back to Victorian music hall when it was popular for females to impersonate men and people also enjoyed seeing their favourite (male) comedian hamming it up as the 'Dame'!

Animals — There is always an animal in the cast, such as Bessie the Cow, Dobbin the good old pantomime horse or Puss in Boots. Someone called Charlie Chaplin once played the back end of a pantomime horse – he went on to become a very famous actor in silent films.

Sweets — For many years, at some point in a pantomime, sweets have been thrown into the audience. Sadly, this is now often stopped for health and safety reasons!

The Season — Pantomimes are traditionally put on around the Christmas season, but can be staged at any time of year.

The Stars — Many celebrities now spend their Christmasses starring in pantomimes up and down the country.

* Stage left is the actor's left as they stand on the stage facing the audience, similarly, stage right is the actor's right as they face the audience.

CONTENTS

TEACHER'S NOTES

Synopsis	4
Song Synopsis and Performance Tips	5
Cast List	6
Casting Tips	7
Costume Suggestions	8
Staging Notes	8
Script	9
Licence and Copyright Details	84

THE SONGS

	Music	Lyrics	CD Tracks
Tonight's The Night	24	73	1/12
A Friend Like You	29	74	2/13
It's Not All It's Cracked Up To Be	34	75	3/14
I'm So In Love With Me!	39	76	4/15
You're Going To The Ball	42	77	5/16 & 22
There's A Party Here Tonight	48	78	6/17
A Ton Of Love	52	79	7/18
If I Had One Wish	55	80	8/19
Your Feet Are Too Big!	62	81	9/20
Happy Ever Afters	66	83	10/21

Keep an eye on our website (www.outoftheark.com) for updates and resources for this, and all our other publications.

SYNOPSIS

With audience participation from the outset – goodies to cheer, baddies to boo – and some very corny jokes, the stage is set for the tale of Cinderella to unfold in a vibrant panto-style production. In the rousing opening number **Tonight's The Night**, we learn that Rockerfella is coming to town. For one night only, the artist formerly known as Prince Charming is appearing live in concert and the town is brimming with anticipation and excitement! Sadly, the lovely Cinderella can't go – she has been given far too much to do by her mean sisters. However, she finds consolation in the company of her good friend Buttons as they celebrate their friendship and recall the fun times they've had together in the charming duet, **A Friend Like You**.

Meanwhile, somewhere uptown surrounded by an entourage of hangers-on, we encounter a disenchanted Rockerfella (Rocky), who yearns to be free from the shackles of fame and to find true love with the girl of his dreams. Despite the attempts of his manager Dan Deeny to persuade him not to throw away his career, Rocky decides to abandon his celebrity lifestyle having found that **It's Not All It's Cracked Up To Be**.

As the saying goes, 'the path of true love doesn't always run smoothly' and it is further hampered by the cunning Fairy Nastyboots and her Naughty Kitty *(Boo!)* who are keen to thwart any possible romance! Fairy NB hatches a plan to bring misery to Cinders, but the welly-wearing Fairy Brigade (in a bid to win their wings by ensuring a happy ending) thankfully avert disaster, giving the power of speech to Buttons' dog, Teaser – who, with the help of the audience, foils the rotten plan. *(Hurray!)*

An essential element in any panto is, of course, the 'dame' character(s). Cinderella's stepsisters, Anastacia (Nasty) and Augustina (Gusty), provide us with a wonderfully humorous vignette in their duet **I'm So In Love With Me!** When they receive three invitations (via First Class Male!) to an after concert ball, they tear up Cinderella's and give her even more work to do, leaving her feeling momentarily despondent. She is soon cheered by the appearance of her Fairy Godmother, who together with the Fairy Brigade, orchestrates a magnificent makeover in the magical **You're Going To The Ball**. And so, Act One ends with a radiant Cinderella leaving in a stretch limo, with exhortations to be back before the magic wears off at midnight!

Act Two finds us at the after concert ball, with everyone participating in a lively dance number **There's A Party Here Tonight**, Cinderella and Rockerfella meet and fall in love and all looks promising until once again Fairy Nastyboots gets up to her old tricks – this time putting the clock back one hour in an attempt to humiliate Cinderella in front of Rocky. In the nick of time, Fairy Nuff (leader of the Fairy Brigade) arrives and restores order just as midnight begins to chime! Cinderella rushes out leaving behind a dainty glass slipper, which Rocky finds. Desperate to find her again, he vows to marry the girl whose foot the slipper fits. So sure is he that she is his true love, he orders preparations to be made for their wedding!

Top of the list is, of course, a wedding cake, to be made by the town's finest baker, Monsieur Bunn (aided and abetted by Anastacia, Augustina and some apprentice bakers). The cake is prepared with only the finest ingredients – trust, grace, hugs – and of course **A Ton Of Love**.

The town is once again a hive of activity, with a talent contest arranged by Dan Deeny to find the 'NBT' (Next Big Thing). This is closely followed by a shoe fitting session for Rocky to find his dainty-footed love. Cinders, hearing of Rocky's plan, dares to believe that perhaps her dreams can come true and she prepares to go and try on the shoe. Yet again, Fairy Nastyboots tries her best to ensure an unhappy ending by having the two sisters lock Cinders in the cellar! Wondering if they will ever find each other again and longing to be together, (from opposite sides of the stage) our lovelorn couple sing the moving duet **If I Had One Wish**.

With Cinders still in the cellar the shoe fitting session takes place. All the ladies of the town want to try for the chance to be Rocky's bride but despite their best efforts to fit their tootsies into the delicate shoe, the verdict is: **Your Feet Are Too Big!** (sung to the familiar strains of *The Blue Danube Waltz*).

With a little help from Teaser and the audience, Buttons rescues Cinders and she arrives in time to try on the shoe, which is of course a perfect fit.

All's well that ends well! Dan Deeny finds his 'NBT' in 'Buttons and his talking dog, Teaser'; the Fairy Godmother takes on the awesome challenge of making over Cinderella's sisters; and the Fairy Brigade win their wings. As everyone gathers for the finale, Cinderella and Rockerfella appear in all their finery and the cast have an opportunity to take their bows during the toe-tapping song **Happy Ever Afters**.

SONG SYNOPSIS and PERFORMANCE TIPS

TONIGHT'S THE NIGHT [All]
A high-energy curtain-opener. The show's about to begin! The staging and choreography need to reflect the hype and buzz of the pre-concert anticipation. Everyone in town is getting involved. Groups on stage can build up as the song progresses – eg ticket sellers/programme sellers/ice-cream sellers/concert-goers/photographers/journalists etc... *Come and get your tickets to the greatest show in town!*

A FRIEND LIKE YOU [A duet for Cinders and Buttons]
This delightful song of true friendship is sure to win any audience over. Sung to each other, Cinders and Buttons need to 'act out' the lyrics using kitchen equipment as props for maximum impact. For example, a mop for the cowboy's horse, a colander for the knight's helmet, a whisk for a wand. Plenty of scope for great imaginative interpretation!

IT'S NOT ALL IT'S CRACKED UP TO BE [Rockerfella, Dan Deeny and Chorus]
A Greek-style song with solos/duet for Rockerfella and Dan Deeny who 'negotiate' their way through the verses. The chorus requires group dancing from fans/paparazzi/entourage etc. Rocky and Dan Deeny have to sing their own lines against each other. The pace of this song increases throughout, ending in a big crescendo. (Rocky could finish the song with a dramatic gesture – eg tearing down poster.)

I'M SO IN LOVE WITH ME! [The Ugly Sisters' duet]
The big comic number. The two sisters are trying out different clothes in front of the mirror as they sing this one. Plenty of prancing, preening, bosom-bolstering and red-carpet-posing required! Needs 'hamming-up' with extra 'cheese' thrown in. The perfect opportunity for being completely OTT!

YOU'RE GOING TO THE BALL [Solo Fairy Godmother with Fairy Brigade and Chorus]
A classic 'musical theatre' number featuring the Fairy Godmother and her make-over team and plentiful fairy-dust! Cinders is behind the screen for much of this song, but appears in all her glory for the final verse and chorus. *(Should you require a more mature voice for the role of the Fairy Godmother or additional backing vocal support, please use our extra vocal/backing track – CD Track 22.)*

THERE'S A PARTY HERE TONIGHT [All]
The dance-track that's crying out for some serious disco-diva choreography. The instrumental sections lend themselves very well to aspiring dancers who wish to showcase their skills(!), whilst larger groups could learn some simple hand-jive/dance movements. This song needs to open the second act with a swing – full stage, in-your-face fun.

A TON OF LOVE [Baker(s), Ugly Sisters and Chorus]
A real feel-good, fun song – a recipe for success. All the ingredients need to be passed along a long line into an enormous mixing bowl, which is put in the 'oven' at the end of the song. Lots of scope for slapstick dramatisation and creative interpretation. (If you have a second identical mixing bowl already tucked away in the oven, full of confetti, this can be taken out at the end of the song and suitably 'thrown' over the front rows of the audience!)

IF I HAD ONE WISH [Cinderella and Rockerfella]
This is the big heart-rending ballad. Cinderella and Rockerfella are on opposite sides of the stage, unaware of each other as they sing this dreamy duet. (Keep the tissues handy.)

YOUR FEET ARE TOO BIG! [All and audience]
This audience-participation song is written to the melody of *The Blue Danube Waltz* and should engage your audiences instantaneously! (The 'echo' lines can be written out on cards and held up through each of the verses. We recommend that verse 1 is performed as an example before the audience join in for subsequent verses.) Eager women waiting in the queue can be pushing and shoving through the choruses. It would also be great to have one of Rocky's attendants searching for women in the audience, a couple of whom could be taken on stage to try on the slipper.

HAPPY EVER AFTERS [All]
A rousing 'anthemic' grand finale – ideal for jiving/arm-waving and gathering all the cast, in groups, across the stage, ready to take their bows at the very end. See if you can't get your audience on their feet before the conclusion of this song!

CAST LIST

Speaking parts:

Cinderella (Cinders)*	*our rags to riches heroine*
Rockerfella (Rocky)*	*the artist formerly known as Prince Charming*
Anastacia* / Augustina*	*Nasty and Gusty by name and nature*
Dan Deeny*	*Rocky's manager*
Buttons*	*Cinders' best friend, a cheery chap*
Teaser, the dog	*a man's (Buttons') best friend*
Fairy Nastyboots (Fairy NB)	*a nasty piece of work (hiss, boo!)*

Fairy Brigade:
Fairy Nuff
Fairy Cake   *the fairies you can trust with fairy dust (hurray!)*
Fairy Sajollygoodfellow (Fairy Sjf)
Fairy Liquid

Fairy Godmother (Fairy G)*	*a make-over expert*
Offstage Inspector (Offstage Insp)	*interfering busybody*
2 x warm-up people (WP1/WP2)	*the jokers in the pack*
Rocky 2 (for dream sequence)	*day-dreaming boy*
Cinders 2 (for dream sequence)	*the girl of his dreams*
Monsieur Bunn le Baker (M. Bunn)	*the clue's in the name!*
Town Crier	*bell-ringer with a big voice*
Magazine Reporter (Mag Rptr)	*an inquisitive person (Prying Eye)*
PR / Costume	*essential companions for any superstar!*
Paparazzi	*flashy type*
Mirror	*a reflective character*
Bear	*the talkative one of the three (bears)*
Messenger (First Class Male)	*exudes style and confidence*
Programme Seller	*entrepreneurial type – Alan Sugar in his early days*
3 x Townspeople	*one-line wonders*
Footman	*the life and 'sole' of the party*

Non-speaking parts:

Naughty Kitty	*a truly catty individual (lots of acting!)*
Townspeople/party guests/bakers	*the backbone of the piece*
Cinderella's animals	*cute, cute and more cute*
2 x Bears	*the not so talkative two of the three (bears)*
Limo	*a stretching role (see Staging Notes)*
Talent Contest Acts	*Your chance to prove that your school has got talent!*

* Solo singing required

CASTING TIPS

Singing parts (requiring solo singing):

Cinderella/Rockerfella — Traditional heroine/hero. It is important that they have good, strong singing voices, as they will perform key solo parts.

Ugly Sisters — These parts should be played with great gusto by confident children with bags of character and a good sense of humour! Singing voices need to be good enough to carry a duet. It would help enormously if the parts could be played by children who either already have, or could develop, a rapport between them. These 'dame' characters are traditionally played by males, but can be cast equally successfully as females.

Buttons — Again, a good singing voice required and lots of confidence, as this character interacts with the audience.

Fairy Godmother — Slightly eccentric and stately, but warm and kind. This part demands the ability to convey a mature presence and to sing clearly or Cinderella might never realise she has to be home by midnight! As this part could be played equally well by a child or an adult, it might be fun for the children if a member of staff were to rise to the challenge!

Dan Deeny — Rocky's wheeler-dealer manager. Needs to exude an air of authority and success and carry off some solo singing to boot.

Group singing only:

Teaser — Needs to be physically agile enough to perform tricks! Also confident enough to engage with the audience.

Fairy Nastyboots — Strong, 'nasty' voice! Great stage presence and willingness to 'play' the audience and enjoy eliciting 'Boo!'s.

Fairy Brigade — Can be an assorted jumble of characters! They need to be vibrant and lively and able to speak in verse.

Offstage Inspector — Authoritative voice; fairly agile/flexible as there is a degree of leaping around required for this part.

Warm-up people — Very confident, as they prepare the audience and encourage participation from them. Good verse speakers.

Naughty Kitty — Good body/facial expression – lots of miming – no talking but essential character portrayal through actions.

Townspeople/group actors/singers/dancers — The chorus are really important – a strong stage presence from them will make all the difference. Also, as there are several opportunities for choreographed numbers, children who can move rhythmically can have a chance to shine! It might be useful to encourage the non-speaking cast members to develop a 'back story' i.e. to think of a name for their character, an age, etc and to have a story ready (their favourite place to go; first thing they remember eating), to relate to someone else if they're supposed to be chatting/interacting in the background. This will help them to look really animated.

Cinders 2/Rocky 2 — As they take on the roles of Cinders and Rocky in a dream sequence, it would be helpful if they could be of a similar size and build. Their costumes should be identical to those of the main characters.

COSTUME SUGGESTIONS

Overall, the costumes should be fairly traditional:

Cinders	A ragged, dull-coloured, dirty dress with apron and broom. A ball gown as flashy as you can make it – for the ball and finale. The charity shops are a good source for discarded bridesmaid dresses, which can look stunning. A decent wig would be useful because of the short time for her transformation. It could be securely fitted in the interval.
Ugly Sisters	You can let your imagination run riot here! The more outrageous the better! Clashing patterns and colours, big bloomers and lots of padding. Again, charity shops should yield something which can be adapted.
Buttons	Bellboy-type outfit, but any jacket with lots of buttons would be fine, as long as it's nice and bright, reflecting Buttons' personality.
Rocky	Needs to look very 'rock 'n' roll'! A leather jacket and jeans perhaps, and for the finale, a smart suit or a stylish jacket.
Fairy Brigade	Yards of netting! Tutus are relatively easy to make and can go over shorts and T-shirts. Tutus should be white or light pastel colours. Wellies of any description. Wings/ballet shoes or similar for the finale only. Wands of course!
Fairy Godmother	Should look more sophisticated and mature than the other fairies – longer tutu, wings, perhaps a tiara and a posh wand. A slightly eccentric accessory or two such as some flashy spectacles and some large, brightly coloured beads.
Fairy Nastyboots	Traditional fairy gear but in earthy colours i.e. greens, browns, black.
Bakers	Will need aprons and matching baker's hats.
Warm-up people	A 'music hall' feel – brightly coloured outfits.
Mirror	Probably best made from the ubiquitous cardboard covered in silver foil! It can be decorated as elaborately as you wish and either worn sandwich board style or have a hole cut out for the mirror's face, which would then need to be face-painted silver.
Animals	Best done with face paints, ears and tails. It would be a shame to lose facial expression behind masks.
Townspeople	Everyday wear – skirts/blouses/trousers plus evening wear for the ball.

STAGING NOTES

Unless there is a large budget, or an enthusiastic art department, you are probably best creating a single background of a town street and using props, as indicated, to create the other scenes. You could also use cards to denote the different settings, making sure they are large enough to be read and that people have enough time to read them, eg:

CINDER'S KITCHEN	1. 'Bijou Kitchen with many original features. Very cosy!'
	(Followed by) 2. 'Cramped, really old. No room to swing a cat!'
MONSIEUR BUNN LE BAKER'S	'Bunn's Bakery: I make lots of dough'
	'Where you can have your cake and eat it!'
ROCKY'S HOTEL ROOM	'Meanwhile over at the (local town) Hilton...'
	'Rocky's Room: Penthouse Suite for Pent-up Superstar!'
BALLROOM	'Ye Olde Palais Ballroom: Enjoy it now, it will be a Bingo Hall in ten years!'

Limo – this can be created by having two people stand closely together until Cinders is about to get in, at which point they move apart, stretching out some fabric/concertinaed card between them. The person at the front should wear a chauffeur's hat and jacket. The 'rear' end could have a number plate reading 'The End – but only of Act One!'

Fairy Brigade action – any movement with three parts, to coincide with the *"Wey, hey, hey!"*, for example, a twirl, both arms up and wand hand forward for final *"Hey!"*

SCRIPT

ACT ONE

OVERTURE   CD Track 11

This useful track provides a flavour of what's to come and is ideal for gathering the audience before the performance (and also Act Two). No piano music is provided for this track.

SCENE 1

The stage is set as a village street, with a backdrop of shops eg: 'Primark: be a wolf in cheap clothing!'/'Fairy Tiles – all you need for a storybook bathroom'/'Monsieur Bunn le Baker'/Tesco Metro (well they do get everywhere!)/'The Ball's In Your Court! – party planners by royal appointment'. There should be posters announcing Rockerfella's live concert.

Enter two warm up people, dressed very brightly – perhaps large multi-coloured bow ties etc. They have various 'cue cards': Hiss/Boo! etc. They display these throughout the play, as indicated.

WP1	I say, I say, I say. How do rabbits go on holiday?
WP2/Aud	I don't know. How do rabbits go on holiday?
WP1	They fly British Hareways!
WP2	I say, I say, I say. What do you call a teacher with a jokebook on his head?
WP1/Aud	I don't know. What do you call a teacher with a joke book on his head?
WP2	A Tee-hee-cher!
WP1	Well, looks as if you're all awake. We'll just check by asking you to read some cards – see who's been listening in Literacy. Read them out as loudly as you can. OK. *(Hold up cue cards)* Good. *(To WP2)* Do you think they're ready?
WP2	Yes.
WP1	Then the tale of Cinderella we will now begin. It starts off pretty sadly so let's have some violins.

        SFX Violins (quietly)   CD Track 23

Cinders enters with a couple of animals and begins sweeping, stopping every so often to daydream.

WP2	Cinders is a lovely girl who has a heart of gold. Her mean and nasty sisters make her do as she is told – She shops and cooks and washes but they don't pay her a penny, They buy themselves all sorts of treats and don't give Cinders any!
WP1	She's always really good and kind – she rescues poorly pets. But nasty names and piles of dirty clothes are all she gets!
WP2	She dreams of one day finding love; a love that's warm and true. But is that Cinder's destiny? We'll know before we're through!

Cinders and animals exit, WPs move aside.

SFX Baddie music — CD Track 24

Enter Fairy Nastyboots and Naughty Kitty.
Green lights/smoke would be effective here, if available!

Cue Card: Hiss/Boo!

Fairy NB   I am Fairy Nastyboots,
           I'm horrid right down to my roots!
           You think you've come here to have fun –
           To see love's battle fought and won,
           But I'll make sure it ends in tears;
           I'll have my way – never you fear!
           I'll use my wicked fairy wiles
           To take away all cheery smiles.
           With Naughty Kitty helping me,
           I'll bring about catastrophe!
           So hear this message I am sending:
           There'll be no sickly happy ending! Ha ha!

Cue Card: Hiss/Boo!

Exit Fairy Nastyboots and Naughty Kitty.

Enter Fairy Brigade: (Fairy Nuff/Fairy Liquid/Fairy Sajollygoodfellow/Fairy Cake) other side of stage. They wear fairy outfits but with wellies and no wings.

Fairy Nuff   Don't panic – she won't have things all her way.

All   The Fairy Brigade's here with a wey hey hey! *(All do action - see staging directions)*

Cue Card: Hooray!

Each Fairy steps forward, calls out her name and waves.

Fairy Cake   If you're wondering why we're in wellies,
              It's because, the truth to tell is…

Fairy Liquid We must <u>walk</u>, our help to bring,
              For we have yet to win our wings!
              And this will only happen when
              True love conquers once again.

Fairy Sjf   We travel through all sorts of weather
              To bring all those in love together.

Cue Card: Ahh!

Fairy Nuff   So if love's hopes should start to fade,
              Waiting in the wings is the Fairy Brigade!

              That's waiting in the wings over there *(points off)* 'cos we haven't got our own wings to wait in. Not yet. *(Indicates to her back)*

All exit.

SCENE 2

Crowds gather, chattering and excited. There could be various vendors and excited fans with 'We love Rocky' banners etc. Cinderella has a shopping basket and a very long list. She checks in her purse and perhaps looks longingly at a poster for the concert. A town crier enters, ringing his bell.

Town Crier   Hear ye! Hear ye! The ticket office will open in five minutes! Get your tickets here! Rockerfella live in concert! The artist formerly known as Prince Charming! Get your tickets here! Once they're gone, they're gone!

Townsprsn 1	Ooo! I think I'm going to faint! This is the most exciting thing to happen here since… (Mr/s… took over as headteacher/we won Eurovision – add local detail)!
Prog Seller	Get your souvenir programme here! Free cut out Rocky doll with seven outfits! Sell on ebay next week for a huge profit!

SONG 1   **Tonight's The Night** [All] *(See p73 for lyrics)*   CD Track 1/12

Town Crier	Hear ye! Hear ye! The ticket office is now open!

All rush off, except Cinders, Buttons and Teaser. Cinders stands in front of poster, looking miserable. Buttons moves front of stage

Buttons	Hello everyone. My name's Buttons and this is my dog, Teaser. Say hello Teaser.
Teaser	Aaroo!
Buttons	I'm Cinderella's best friend. She doesn't look very happy does she? I'd better go and find out what's wrong. Hello Cinders.
Cinders	*(Walking to the front)* Hello Buttons.
Buttons	You don't look very happy. Aren't you going to the concert tonight?
Cinders	I can't Buttons – look at the list of things my sisters have left for me to do before tonight! *(Produces huge, long list)* Hello Teaser. *(Strokes him)*
Buttons	No wonder they're known as the Ugly Sisters!
Offstage Insp	*(Running on, incensed)* Excuse me, you can't say things like that! *(Teaser growls)*
Buttons	Why not? Who are you?
Offstage Insp	I'm Jack, the <u>Off</u>stage Inspector, and you can't call people ugly. It's just not done!
Buttons	But this is a panto – they're always called the Ugly Sisters! Besides – it's not because of what they look like – it's because the way they <u>behave</u> is so mean and ugly.
Offstage Insp	Sorry, but you just can't say it.
Buttons	Oh yes we can, can't we boys and girls?
Offstage Insp	On no you can't! *(Etc.)*

Fairy Nuff enters side of stage.

Fairy Nuff	I can see this fellow's a bit of a pest. I'll put some fleas inside his vest!

Offstage Insp runs off scratching.

Buttons	Hey Cinders! – An <u>off</u>stage inspector called Jack, Of humour does suffer a lack. Suddenly he starts twitching And scratching and itching. Let's move on before he comes back!

All exit quickly.

SCENE 3

Kitchen scene: needs to be set with lots of equipment – mop, colander, brush, chair, a large jar marked 'Animal Food' and a large empty sack, for use later. To one side is the 'refuge area'. Sign: 'A Frog is for life, not just for dinner!' There are a few animals, including a frog.

Cinders, Buttons and Teaser re-enter. Enter Ugly Sisters, dressed outrageously in cheerleader type outfits, preferably padded out to look as OTT as possible. They have cheerleader pompoms.

Ugly S (Tog)	Hello everyone. We've come to brighten up your day with our wit and beauty!
Buttons	That's the biggest joke I've heard so far!
Anastacia	My name's Anastacia, but my friends call me 'Nasty'.
Augustina	My name's Augustina, but my friends call me 'Gusty'.
Buttons	*(To audience)* I can't think why!
Anastacia	This is a new outfit. Do you think my bottom looks big in this?
Augustina	Oh no dear! *(Anastacia looks smug. Pause)* It looks ginormous!

Enter Mirror.

Anastacia	Mirror, mirror on the wall, who is the fairest of them all?
Mirror	I'm sorry, we're currently experiencing a high volume of calls to this number. Your call is important to us and you will be held in a queue. Thank you for your patience. *(Exit)*
Anastacia	Stupid thing! Oi you! Cindersmella! *(Sisters laugh)* Here's a few more jobs for you, to stop you sitting round, you lazy girl! *(Give Cinders another long list)*
Augustina	We need to practice our little routine to impress Rocky tonight.
Ugly S (Tog)	R – O – C K Y – Rocky boy you've caught my eye. 236452 zero – call me up and be my hero!
Augustina	You need to practice more, you're cramping my style.
Anastacia	It's not me! Your bloomers are too tight!

Sisters exit, still bickering/practising.

Cinders	I suppose I'd better get started on this lot.
Buttons	Come on, I'll give you a hand. You know, Cinders, you and I go together like peaches and cream, fish and chips, _____ school and the best teachers!
Cinders	Ferraris and footballers, knives and forks, Teaser and bones!
Buttons	You've got it! We belong together. Hey! Why don't we make a game of all this work, then it won't seem so bad? Remember how that song goes, something about sugar and medicine…?
Cinders	Oh I know a better song than that!

> **SONG 2**   **A Friend Like You** *(See p74 for lyrics)*   CD Track 2/13
> [Cinders and Buttons]

Each verse could be acted out, using kitchen equipment, eg a colander as shining armour, mop as a horse etc. The animals could help to hand out relevant items.

Cinders	Thank you, Buttons. You always make me feel better.	
Buttons	*(To audience)* I just wish I could make her fall in love with me.	**Cue Card: Ahh!**
Cinders	*(Stroking animals)* I'm so lucky to have such wonderful friends.	

They remain in the background, miming clearing up/sitting chatting etc.

SFX Baddie music   **CD Track 24**

Fairy Nastyboots and Naughty Kitty enter side of stage.   **Cue Card: Hiss/Boo!**

Fairy NB	This cosy friendship makes me sick, True misery's what makes me tick! So I've hatched a brilliant, nasty ruse For Naughty Kitty to use her mews. *(Kitty mews horribly)* To be taken in by <u>kind</u> Cinderella, Then put this poison where I tell 'er And feed it to Cinders' cuddly crew – They'll be <u>dying</u> to eat my deadly brew! Ha, ha, ha, ha.	**Cue Card: Hiss/Boo!**

As they begin to exit...

Offstage Insp	I'm sorry to interrupt, but this is one of those times – I must complain about some of those rhymes.
Fairy Cake	*(Enters opp side of stage)* This fellow is going from bad to verse! I'll give him some 'time-out' with the three bears. *(Bears run on and take him off)*
Offstage Insp	What are you doing? You can't do this, it's the wrong fairytale!
Bear	*(Whilst taking him off)* When I said I wanted an important, moving part, this wasn't what I meant.
Fairy Cake	On Naughty Kitty we'll keep an eye, She'll be up to no good, by and by!

All exit.

SCENE 4

Rocky's room. There are lots of hangers-on: Magazine Reporter, PR, Costume, Paparazzi, Bodyguards, Make-Up etc. Dan Deeny, Rocky's manager, is on the phone arranging more bookings (improvise). Large reviews displayed: 'Rocky rocks 'em!', 'The artist formerly known as Prince Charming gives a right royal performance!'

Mag Rptr	So, Rocky, I'm from Howdy magazine. Your fans want to know everything about you and I mean everything! You're public property now, you know. If you could just answer a few questions: What do you eat for breakfast? Something yummy I hope, as our readers will no doubt copy you. How many girlfriends have you had? Have you ever had a pet? What was it called?
PR	Rocky has Chocopops for breakfast, he works far too hard to have time for girlfriends and he once had a very cute cat called Rover. That's all for now thank you.
Rocky	A cat called Rover! I've never had a cat in my life! And I can't stand Chocopops!
PR	That's all very well, but you have a promotion deal with them so you'll have to be seen eating them now and again.

Costume	You are going to look the business in this. It positively shrieks S. T. A .R! *(Holds up some sort of hideous creation)* If you could try it on, we'll see if it needs any tweaking.
Paparazzi	OK, let's have some poses for the photo shoot: give me thinking man; mean and moody; lost in thought. *(Rocky is)* OK, lovely. Now let's do... Rocky! Rocky!
Rocky	*(Suddenly becoming animated)* I'm sorry, Dan. I've been thinking. I can't do this anymore! I just want to be ordinary and free to fall in love with the girl of my dreams!

All freeze in comical positions. Rocky in a dreamy pose, Dan and others looking shocked. A second Rocky and Cinders, dressed in the same outfits as their matching character, enter in slo-mo – with suitable music if possible. They meet centre stage.

Rocky 2	Hello. I think I love you.
Cinders 2	I bet you say that to all the girls you meet in your dreams.
Rocky 2	I've never met a girl in my dreams before.
Cinders 2	I've never been in anyone's dream before.
Rocky 2	Wow! That must mean we're meant for each other. Let's go for a walk.

As they exit, all unfreeze.

Rocky	I've made my mind up; this will be my last concert! I'm going to go back to being plain old Prince Charming. I thought this rock star celebrity stuff was what I wanted, but it's not all it's cracked up to be.
Dan Deeny	Oh come on now Rocky – don't throw it all away! I don't want to be the one who's gonna have to beg you to stay...

SONG 3 **It's Not All It's Cracked Up To Be** *(See p75 for lyrics)* CD Track 3/14
[Rocky/Dan/Entourage]

Rocky	Sorry Dan, but my mind's made up. I will help you find the NBT if you like.
All	NBT? What's that?
Rocky/Dan	The Next Big Thing, of course!

Exit.

SCENE 5

Cinders kitchen/refuge, as before. Cinders is there with her animals.

Cinders	Right you lot, time for a nap. *(To Frog)* Oh Freddo, fancy somebody abandoning you just because you didn't turn into a handsome prince when they kissed you! I'll find you a nice, new home with someone who'll value you just for being you – all green and squishy. *(Animals exit, except Teaser)*
	Come on, Teaser, let's practice some of your tricks. Down! Roll over! Beg! *(Does hands together, pleading pose)* Good boy! You're so clever. *(Awful caterwauling is heard)* Whatever is that? It sounds like my sisters singing in the shower, but they're out shopping.

Enter Naughty Kitty carrying an empty lunchbox.

Cinders	Oh look! It's a poor little kitty cat. What have you got there? A lunchbox. But it's empty! It should be full of nourishing, healthy goodies! Let me get you something to eat. Oh no! Our jar is empty! I've got a few pennies left. I'll go and buy something right now. You lie down there and have a nap. Look after her, Teaser.

Kitty lies down and pretends to nap. So does Teaser. Enter Fairy Liquid and Fairy Sajollygoodfellow side of stage.

Fairy Liquid	The emergency service you can trust! The Fairy Brigade with some fairy dust!	**Cue Card: Hooray!**
Fairy Sjf	That naughty Kitty a lesson we'll teach By giving Teaser the gift of speech!	

They sprinkle dust on Teaser and exit.

SFX Fairy   CD Track 25

Teaser	Helloooo boys and girls. Hey, it's good to talk! I'll just make sure you can understand me. Knock, knock.
Audience	Who's there?
Teaser	Felix.
Audience	Felix who?
Teaser	Felix my lolly, I'll go mad! Listen, I don't trust that Kitty. I'm going to go and hide all my bones somewhere safe. If she gets up to any mischief, will you call me? Shout out: 'Here Teaser. Here boy'. Can you do that? Let's have a little practice...

As soon as Teaser goes off, Kitty wakes up and begins to sneak over to the food jar with bottle of poison. **SFX Creeping music (CD Track 26) (Cue Card: Hiss/Boo)** *Teaser comes on* **(Cue Card: Behind You)** *and to shouts of 'Behind you!' he turns round, but Kitty manages to stay behind him. Repeat a couple of times. Teaser eventually sees Kitty, gets large sack and pops it over her head and takes her off.*

Teaser	*(To audience, making 'shh' gesture)* Now don't you lot go letting the cat out of the bag.
Cinders	*(Entering)* Here kitty, kitty. Oh where did she go? And Teaser's disappeared too! Kitty! Teaser! I don't know. *(To audience)* Never work with children or animals! *(Exit)*

Mirror and Ugly Sisters enter. Anastacia is dressed in an apron and Augustina in gardening gear. Ugly Sisters also bring on basket of clothes which they try on during Song 4.

Anastacia	I do enjoy my cooking lessons at Monsieur Bunn le Baker. His assistant Carl is in lurve with me. He says I give him heartache.
Augustina	He meant heart<u>burn</u>, after eating one of your rock cakes! They used the rest to build a new rockery! <u>I've</u> grown something big and colourful, all yellow and red.
Anastacia	So you have – that huge spot on your chin!
Augustina	Ooh! You're just jealous because I've got green fingers.
Anastacia	Only because you're always picking your nose! Carl says I've got skin like a baby.
Augustina	Yes dear, a baby rhinoceros!

SONG 4**I'm So In Love With Me!** [Ugly Sisters] *(See p76 for lyrics)* CD Track 4/15

Exit.

SCENE 6

Village street. Enter Town Crier, townspeople and Buttons.

Town Crier   Hear ye! Hear ye! Talent contest later! Dan Deeny looking for the NBT!

Townsprsn 2   Hey, at last we can prove that .... *(locality)*'s got talent! Buttons – you could do some of your limericks.

Buttons   Yeah! What about this one?:

A <u>cent</u>ipede called Little John
Was <u>lunch</u>ing with friends prompt at one,
But he got there so late,
Everything had been ate,
He <u>took</u> so long putting shoes on!

I'm going to go and tell Cinderella about the contest. See you later. *(Exit)*

Townsprsn 3   Bye Buttons.

All exit.

SCENE 7

Cinders kitchen. Cinders sits sewing with animals around her. Buttons runs in, excited.

Cinders   Nearly finished. I'm so glad I've got so many lovely friends to keep me company. *(Sounding weary)* Hello Buttons. It's nice to see you.

Buttons   *(Very energetically)* ...to see me, nice! Oh poor Cinders. You look as tired as a Year 6 teacher after SATS!

Fairy Nuff   *(Entering side of stage)* Our Cinders is worn out,
She's looking very pale.
Ooh! What is that arriving...
By First Class Male?

Messenger swaggers on wearing First Class Male sash.

Messenger   3 tickets for the After Concert Ball tonight. All lovely ladies welcome!

As he goes to give them to Cinderella the Ugly Sisters run in and grab them! He takes one look at them, screams and runs off.

Buttons   *(To audience)* One day Nasty and Gusty were all
Set to go to a fancy dress ball,
So that pair of old crones
Thought they'd dress up as bones
And the dog ate them up in the hall!

Anastacia   *(Gives ticket to Augustina)* One for you, one for me. *(Tears up a ticket – to Cinders)* You won't be needing this. You'll be far too busy doing this lot!

They bring on large laundry basket with large bloomers etc in, then exit, chattering excitedly.

Cinders   Oh Buttons! Why do they always have to be so horrid?

Buttons	I'll run after the messenger and see if he's got an extra ticket. *(Exit)*
Cinders	At least I've got all of you – and my dreams! I just wish I could have gone to the ball! Mind you, I don't have anything to wear. Hey! Maybe I could wear these – they'd certainly get me noticed. *(Picks up bloomers and waltzes around with them)*

Enter Mirror, Fairy Godmother and Fairy Brigade, bringing on screen and 'Fairytale Make-over Kit' Initially Cinders doesn't notice them.

Fairy Nuff	Dear Cinders won't need those big knickers. What we've planned is something far slicker.
Fairy Cake	We've been able at last to discover Where to find Cinder's Fairy Godmother.
Fairy Liquid	With her help and the Fairy brigade She'll put all other girls in the shade. *(Coughs)* Ahem!
Cinders	Oh my goodness! Who are you?
Fairy G	I'm the one who's come to make your dreams come true.
Cinders	I don't know what to think. I'm all in a daze.
Fairy G	Then just stand there and be amazed. My dear, for your information We've come to do a transformation!
Cinders	*(Rubbing her eyes)* I think I must be dreaming.
Fairy G	*(Walks around Cinders, taking stock)* For you I'm thinking baby blue... *(Others get items ready)* And something glassy in a shoe. Important to accessorize In colours that bring out your eyes. *(To Fairy)* Let's have those earrings, I think... Your hairstyle really ought to say This is a very special day. We need a look that's not bizarre But leaves no doubt of who you are! Chop, chop everybody – no time to waste. We've got to get this girl ready for the ball!
Cinders	The ball!
Fairy G	Well of course, my dear. You don't think I'd waste my time and talents on any old event do you?!

SONG 5   **You're Going To The Ball** *(See p77 for lyrics)*   CD Track 5/16 or 22
[Fairy Godmother and Fairy Brigade]

At end Cinders exits in stretch limo (see staging notes).

END OF ACT ONE
(There should be at least a short interval to change set)

ACT TWO

SCENE 1

Ballroom with large clock, front of stage, which could be manned. Guests gather in small groups and mime chatting. Town Crier is at side of stage.

WP1	Once again the stage is set, our story's underway. The concert was a huge success – a shame you couldn't stay! (Well, you didn't expect to get a concert as well for the price of these tickets, did you?)
WP2	Cinderella <u>will</u> go to the ball, her beauty quite unique. If those Ugly Sisters spot her tho', they'll have a fit of pique!
WP1	Fairy Nastyboot's plan was truly foiled; she's feeling very vexed! But enough now of this chatter! – Let's see what happens next!

SFX Baddie music   CD Track 24

Enter Fairy Nastyboots and Kitty. Cast freeze as Fairy Nastyboots speaks.

Fairy NB	Fairy Nastyboots is back!	**Cue Card: Hiss/Boo!**
	I've rescued Kitty from the sack,	
	<u>My</u> plan A may have been thwarted	
	But now I have plan <u>B</u> all sorted.	
	I'll put this clock <u>one</u> <u>hour</u> behind *(She does)*	
	And Cinderella soon will find	
	All hopes of true love will be shattered	
	When her prince sees her in filthy tatters! Ha, ha!	**Cue Card: Hiss/Boo!**

Exit Fairy Nastyboots and Kitty. Cast unfreeze.

Town Crier	*(Announcing a few more guests)* Mr and Mrs O'Doors and their daughter, Patty. Mr and Mrs Ball and their daughter, Katya. Mr and Mrs Eckerslike and their son, Willie. The Princess Incognito.

Cinders enters.

                     Hear ye! Hear ye! It's time to partee!

SONG 6   **There's A Party Here Tonight** [All] *(See p78 for lyrics)*   CD Track 6/17

This is a great opportunity for some group choreography – hand jive or similar. At end everybody mill about and **SFX: Love across a crowded room (CD Track 27)**. *Rocky and Cinders move towards each other in slo-mo. When SFX stops, they jolt into life.*

Rocky	Hello. Do you come here often?
Cinders	Not really, this is the first ball there's been here since 1980!
Rocky	Don't I know you? Didn't I walk with you once upon a dream…?
Cinders	You're not very good with chat up lines are you?
Town Crier	Hear ye! Hear ye! The buffet is served!

All except Cinders and Rocky rush off.

Cinders	Shall we dine?

18

Rocky	I could just feast on the sight of you!

Both exit. Offstage Insp enters.

Offstage Insp	Wait a minute! That dialogue is an insult to the audience's intelligence! *(Looks around audience)* Well – some of them! Come back here.
Fairy Nuff	*(Entering)* This fellow is going to spoil our romance! This time let's try some ants in his pants!

Offstage Insp runs off a-leaping followed by Fairy Nuff. Cinders and Rocky re-enter.

Cinders	I must keep an eye on the time.
Rocky	I think it's the most beautiful eye in the world.
Cinders	Oh it's only five to eleven. I can't believe it – it's as if everything's in slow motion when I'm with you.
Fairy Nuff	*(Runs on, breathless)* Oops! Just in time! There was such a big queue for the ladies in the interval and I can't run in wellies! This job will be so much easier with wings. Right: Midnight is nigh, so without much ado, Clock go back to the time that's true! *(It does or Fairy Nuff moves it!)*

SFX Fairy   **CD Track 25**

Cinders	Oh no! Does that clock say nearly midnight?
Rocky	You must tell me your name.
Cinders	Betta be gone!

Chimes start. Cinders runs off, leaving behind a shoe.

Rocky	Betta! Wait! Come back! What's this? She's left a shoe! Don't worry, I'll find you, Betta! Dan! Dan! *(Dan runs on)* Whoever this shoe fits is the girl I'm going to marry! Get those PR people to make themselves useful – put the word out something's a foot; and make some wedding arrangements – when I find my dream girl, I'm not going to lose her again!

All exit.

SCENE 2

Monsieur Bunn le Baker and Ugly Sisters enter. There could also be a group of trainee bakers, who will join in the chorus of the song.

M. Bunn	Rockerfella 'as ordered the most splendid wedding cake ever made. It is to 'ave a model of 'im and 'is bride on top.
Anastacia	That's going to be me!
M. Bunn	Zen perhaps I 'ad better order a couple more tons of icing sugar!
Anastacia	I always knew I was destined for bigger things.
Augustina	Your bottom certainly seems to be!
M. Bunn	Ladies please! We need to get started. I'm going to need plenty of help with this. A wedding cake is a tricky thing to get right.

SONG 7   **A Ton Of Love** *(See p79 for lyrics)*   CD Track 7/18
[Monsieur Bunn, Ugly Sisters, chorus]

Chorus could be group of trainee bakers in hats, who join in the chorus and pass ingredients along 'production line'. There could be some impromptu percussion, using saucepan played with whisk/cheese grater played as a washboard, etc. All exit at end.

SCENE 3

Cinders' kitchen. Cinders (back in rags) is seated, with various animals around her feet.

Cinders	Oh it was such a wonderful evening! But now I'm back to where I was – in filthy tatters! He'd never want me now; life's not like that. He's probably forgotten all about me and gone away. Far, far away.
Town Crier	*(Walking across stage)* Hear ye! Hear ye! Shoe left behind at ball last night! Rockerfella in search of perfect foot for a perfect fit!
Cinders	My shoe! Did you hear that everyone? He *is* trying to find me. Maybe my dreams are all about to come true! I need to smarten myself up a bit.

In Disney-style pastiche, animals brush her hair, tie ribbons etc while Cinders hums.

*Fairy Nastyboots enters side of stage (**SFX Baddie music (CD track 24)** and **Hiss/Boo!** cue card).*

Fairy NB	Newt's teeth! This could be my last chance To destroy all hope for this romance. *(Thinks then has an 'Aha!' moment)* There's plenty of space in her sisters' heads To drop in an idea to stop it dead. I'll bring to mind their dank, dark cellar Where they could lock up Cinderella! Ha, ha! **Cue Card: Hiss/Boo!**

Enter Ugly Sisters.

Anastacia	*(To Cinderella)* What are you looking so happy about you little upstart?
Augustina	Yes! Go and prepare us a foot spa. We've got an important appointment.
Cinders	I'd like to go and try on the shoe too.
Ugly S (Tog)	You! *(Holding their noses)* Phew!
Augustina	It would need to be disinfected if you tried it on. I don't think so!

SFX Fairy   CD Track 25

Ugly S (Tog)	I've just had a wonderful idea! *(Pause)* Cinder-cellar! *(Laugh)*
Cinders	No! Please!

They take Cinders and throw her to one side of the stage (FOS) as if to cellar, then exit. Rocky enters other side of stage.

Rocky	Oh Betta! Where could you be? I had you there and then I let you go. I wonder if we'll ever be together again!

SONG 8   **If I Had One Wish** [Cinders and Rocky] *(See p80 for lyrics)* **CD Track 8/19**

At end Rocky and Cinders both exit. Teaser enters.

Teaser   Hello boys and girls. Have you seen Cinderella anywhere? My master, Buttons, is looking for her. What? She's in the cellar? I'd better go and get Buttons right away! I may be able to talk but I still can't turn keys with my paws! *(Exit)*

SCENE 4

Village street with table and chairs for Rocky/Dan. This is an opportunity for children to show off their party pieces, or there could be a succession of acts coming on and being summarily sent off with cries of 'next!'

Dan Deeny   I hope we have more luck finding your 'Betta' half, Rocky. I just haven't seen anything really different. There's only one more on our list, Buttons. *(Calls)* Buttons! Buttons!

Townsprsn 2   He left a minute ago. He said he had to go and find a friend.

Dan Deeny   Well I'm sorry, but I haven't got time to waste. I think I'll move on to ....*(local town)* – I hear there's loads of talent there. Let's see if we have any 'betta' luck finding your foot!

All exit.

SCENE 5

Same village street, with a single chair beside which ladies are beginning to gather. Enter Town Crier, wearing only one shoe.

Town Crier   Hear ye! Hear ye! Walk this way for the shoe fitting session!

He hops over to chair, holding up shoeless foot. Others follow, doing likewise. Enter Rocky, Dan, footman and entourage and shoe fitting begins. Enter Ugly Sisters.

Anastacia   It took me so long to paint my toenails.

Augustina   And about two tins of emulsion I should think!

Anastacia   Carl just said he thought I looked like Angelina Jolie.

Augustina   You need to get your ears cleaned out – he said he'd like an orange jelly!

PR   Form an orderly queue, please. Who's first?

Anastacia   *(Pushing to front)* Me!

Augustina   That's all right, dear. Age before beauty!

Footman   *(Trying to put shoe on Anastacia's foot, puffing and panting)* I don't think this is going to work, Madame. It's like trying to squeeze an elephant into a tube of Smarties!

SONG 9   **Your Feet Are Too Big!** [All] *(See p81 for lyrics)*   **CD Track 9/20**

This song provides an opportunity to encourage the audience to join in the later choruses. Warm-up people could have cue cards to help with the words.

During instrumental verse:

Rocky   *(Calling out)* Is there anyone else?

Town Crier   *(Calling even louder)* Anyone else?

Ugly S (Tog)   Oh no there isn't! Let <u>me</u> try again. *(They both try to get back to the chair)*

Rocky   Looks like that's it then, everyone.

PR   Never mind Rocky, there's plenty more feet in the street. Go on tour and check out all the feet abroad.

Ugly S (Tog)   I've got broad feet!

Buttons and Cinders run on.

Buttons   Wait! There's one more! Cinderella! *(She tries on shoe)*

Rocky   It fits! There, that's Betta!

Cinders   Oh thank you Buttons!

Dan Deeny   So you're Buttons! Shame you missed your audition.

Cinders   He was rescuing me. Can't you give him another chance Mr Deeny?

Dan Deeny   Oh go on then – what can you do?

Buttons   Once an artist who's called Rockerfella
               Fell in love with our own Cinderella.
               So applaud to the rafters,
               Hap-pill-lee ever afters,
               Because nothing could be much more swella!

Cinders/Rocky exit to change.

Offstage Insp runs on but Dan puts a hand over his mouth before he can speak.

Dan Deeny   That's very good Buttons, but I'm really looking for...

Buttons   ...and I've got a very special dog. Here Teaser. Sit! Roll over! *(Etc)*

Dan Deeny   Very cute – just not very original.

Teaser   Would you like me to tell a joke then?

Dan Deeny   Thanks for offering, but... what did you say?

Teaser   I said 'would you like me to tell a joke?'

Dan Deeny   Who said that?

Teaser   Helloo! *(Holding up paws)* Paws for thought. Who do you think said it? Me of course!

Dan Deeny   Rocking robins! I think I've found the NBT! Buttons and his amazing talking dog!

Teaser   That sounds good, but we'll have to see about the billing.

Fairy Brigade enter with their wings and ballet shoes (or similar) to replace wellies.

Fairy cake	So all ends happily and we have got our wings! All that remains is to celebrate a sweet exchange of rings.	**Cue Card: Hooray!**
Fairy Sjf	We've even got left over here some special fairy dust, Let's use it to transform Nastyboots and her mean old puss!	
	SFX Fairy	**CD Track 25**
Fairy NB	I feel all warm and cuddly, I could give someone a hug.	
Offstage Insp	I'll throw away my rule book And we'll be like bugs in a rug! *(They hug)*	
Fairy G	I'm looking for a make-over project, A real challenge would be nice. *(Spots Ugly Sisters)* You two look perfect for the task, I'll get to do it twice!	
Buttons	An offstage inspector one day Happened to come to our play. When his verdict he gave, He did nothing but rave, And the fairies all went...	
Fairy Brigade	Wey hey hey! *(Action)*	

Cinders and Rocky re-appear.   **Cue Card: Hooray!**

        SONG 10   **Happy Ever Afters** [All] *(See p83 for lyrics)*   **CD Track 10/21**

THE END

TONIGHT'S THE NIGHT

(All)

*[Prog Seller: Get your souvenir programme here! Free cut out Rocky doll with seven outfits!
Sell on ebay next week for a huge profit!]*

1. To-

-night's the night! At last the moment's ar-
(2.) -night's the night! The cur-tain's rea-dy to
(3.) -night's the night! We're gon-na head for the

Words and Music by Mark and Helen Johnson
© 2008 Out of the Ark Ltd, Middlesex TW12 2HD
CCLI Song No. 5183845

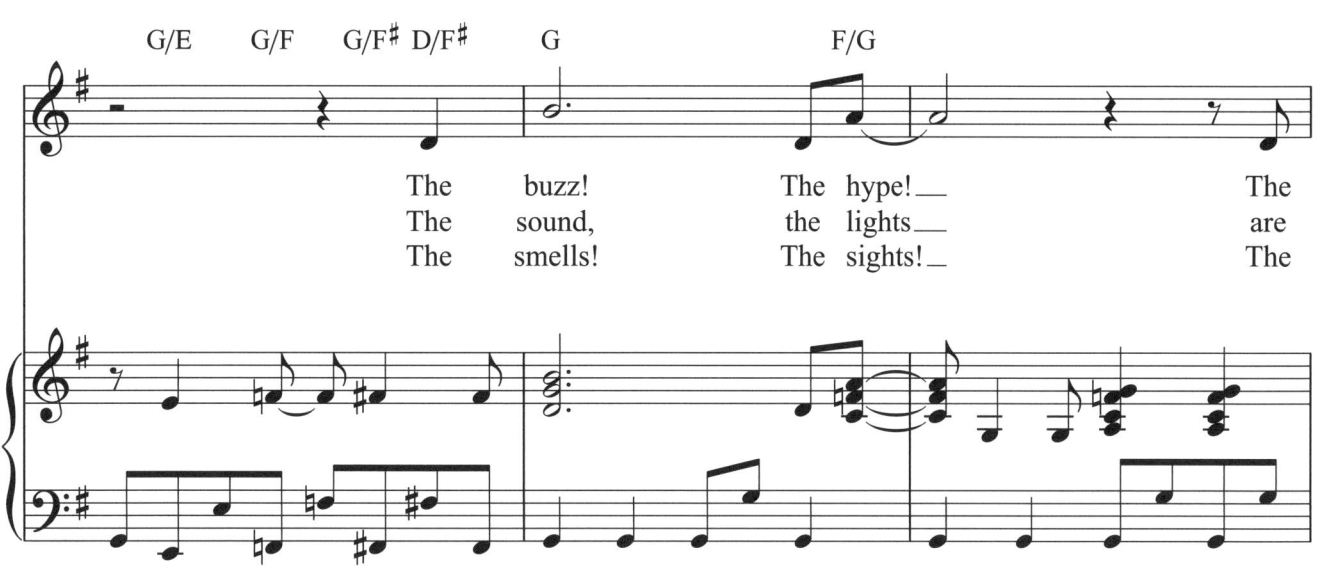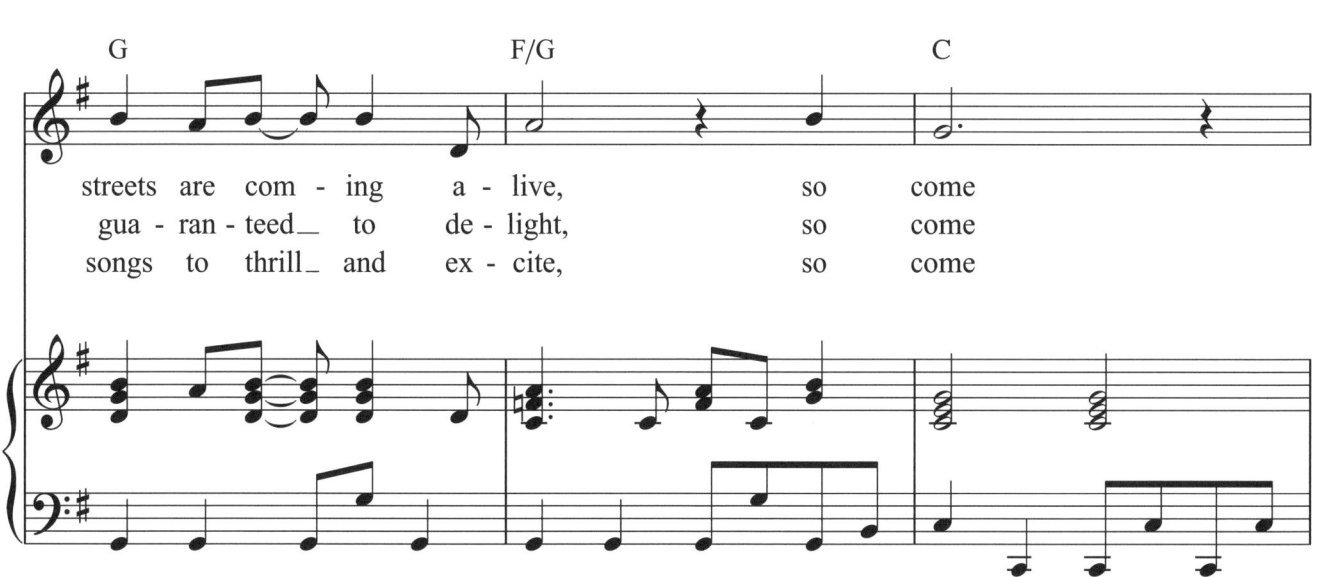

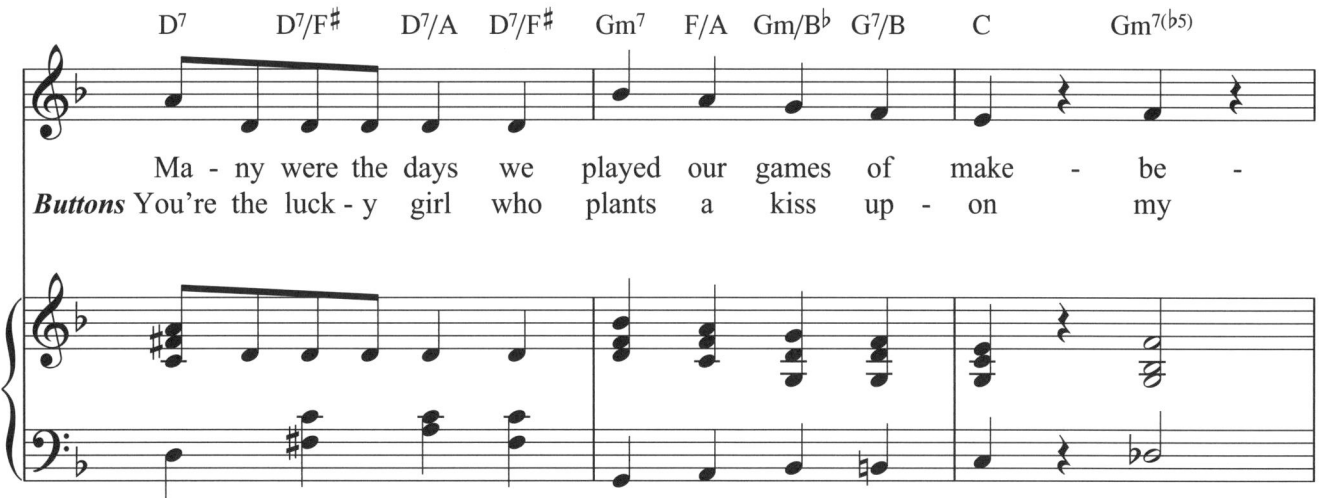
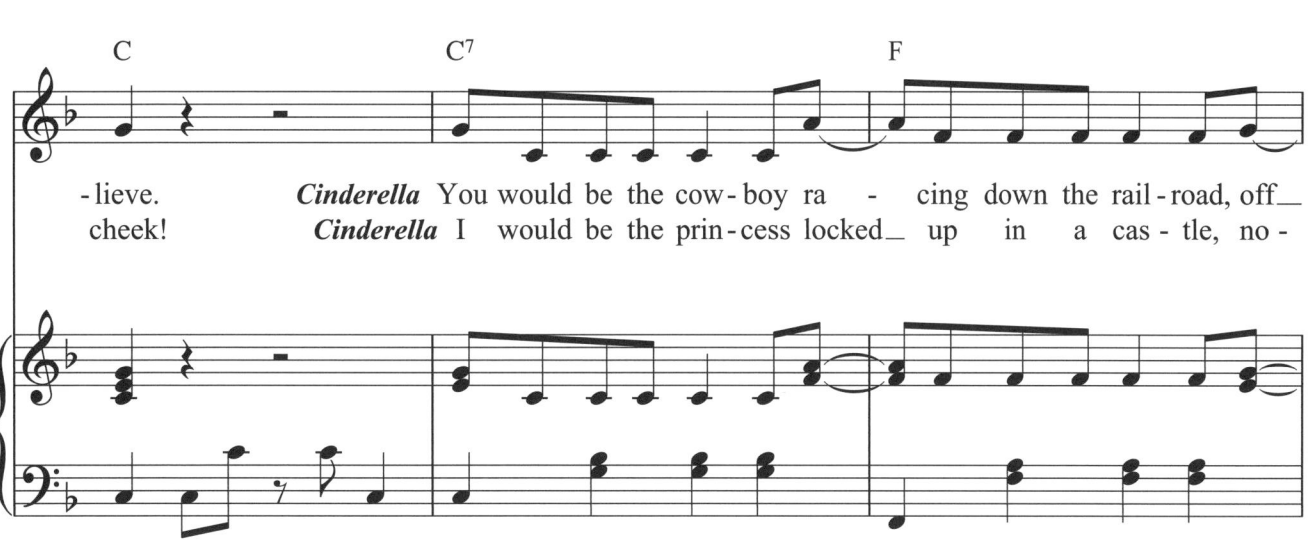

IT'S NOT ALL IT'S CRACKED UP TO BE

(Rockerfella, Dan Deeny and Chorus)

[Dan Deeny: Oh come on now Rocky – don't throw it all away! I don't want to be the one who's gonna have to beg you to stay...]

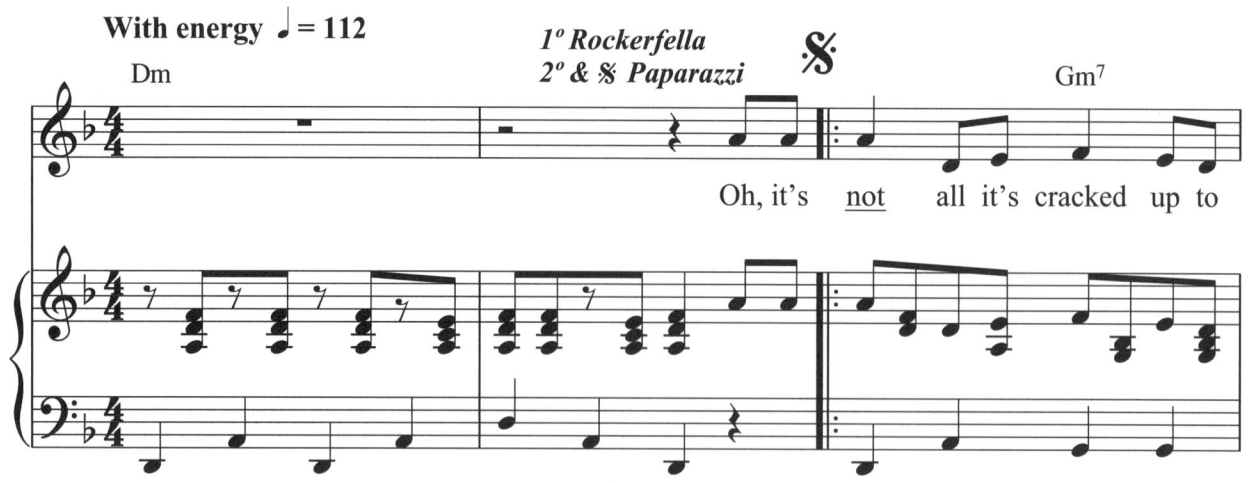

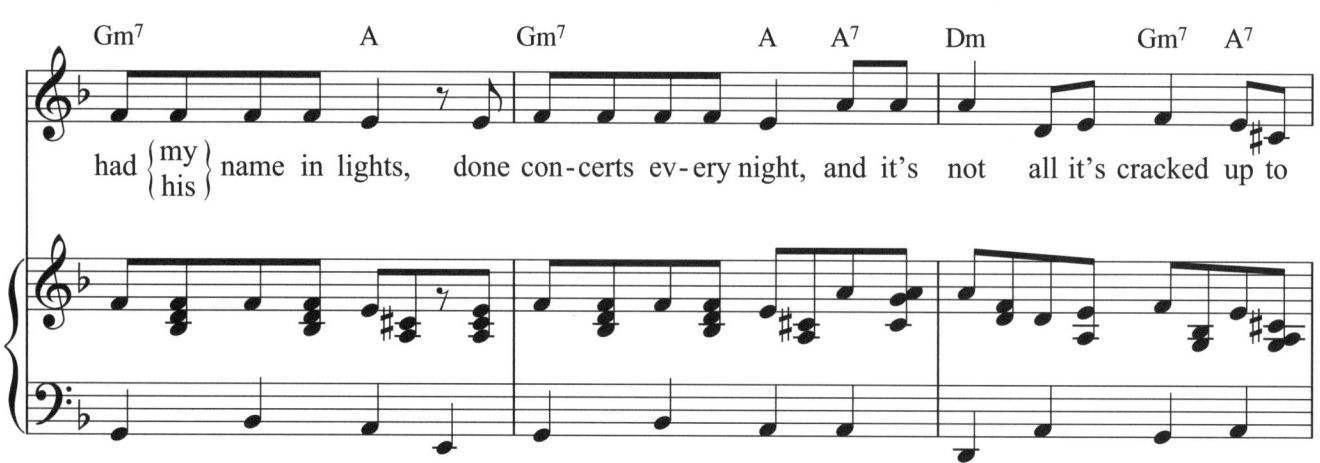

Words and Music by Mark and Helen Johnson
© 2008 Out of the Ark Ltd, Middlesex TW12 2HD
CCLI Song No. 5183869

con-certs ev-ery night, and it's not all it's cracked up to be! 2. I

1. *Dan Deeny*

2. be!

Dan Deeny I can't be-lieve you'd throw it all a-way!

May-be you need to take a ho-li-day. You're just a lit-tle stressed, so

D.S. al Coda

get your-self a rest. Come to your sen-ses and we'll talk a-gain! Oh it's *Paparazzi*

CODA
1° only

Dan: I can't believe you'd throw it all a-way! May-be you need to take a ho-li-day. You're just a lit-tle stressed, so get your-self a rest. Come to your sen-ses and we'll talk a-gain!

Paprzi. *(both times)*: not all it's cracked up to be! He's lived a life of fame and ce-le-bri-ty. He's had his name in lights, done con-certs ev-ery night, and it's not all it's cracked up to be! Oh it's be!

I'M SO IN LOVE WITH ME!

(Ugly Sisters)

[Anastacia: Only because you're always picking your nose! Carl says I've got skin like a baby.
Augustina: Yes dear, a baby rhinoceros!]

Steadily ($\sqrt{} = \sqrt{}\sqrt{}$) ♩ = 126

Anastacia (Anas.)
Augustina (Aug.)

Anas. 1. How could a-ny-bo-dy think we're sis-ters?
Aug. 2. Would you say my bot-tom looks e-nor-mous?
Anas. 3. Sing a song of 'Hap-py Ev-er Af-ter',
Aug. 4. One day I'll be Mrs Roc-ker-fel-la,

Aug. It's a to-tal mys-ter-y to me! Anas. My dain-ty feet!
Should I try a brigh-ter shade of green? I can't de-cide!
Aug. Sing a song of 'Will You Mar-ry Me?' Anas. Whisked off my feet,
Anas. One day you'll be mar-ried– in your dreams! Aug. I'll be the bride!

Words and Music by Mark and Helen Johnson
© 2008 Out of the Ark Ltd, Middlesex TW12 2HD
CCLI Song No. 5183876

Aug. My ro-sy cheeks! *Both* How could a-ny poor old man re-sist us!?
Anas. Take my ad-vice, close your eyes and say "I'm look-ing gor-geous!"
Aug. held cheek to cheek, *Both* ho-ney-moon in sun-ny Cos-ta Bra-va!
Anas. I'd be sur-prised! *Both* Hand-in-hand we'll walk the aisle to-ge-ther.

Anas. May-be I should try a brigh-ter lip-stick?
Aug. Blow a kiss in front of all the cam-eras,
Anas. See me rub-bing shoul-ders with the film stars,
Aug. Think of Fred A-staire and Gin-ger Ro-gers,

Aug. May-be add a tub of wrin-kle cream! *Both* I'm on a quest to
Anas. we'll be ev-ery-thing they want to see! *Both* Fel-las will all be
Aug. see my face in 'Hel-lo' ma-ga-zine. *Both* Time to move o-ver
Anas. more like twee-dle-dum and twee-dle-dee! *Both* Don't I de-serve a

40

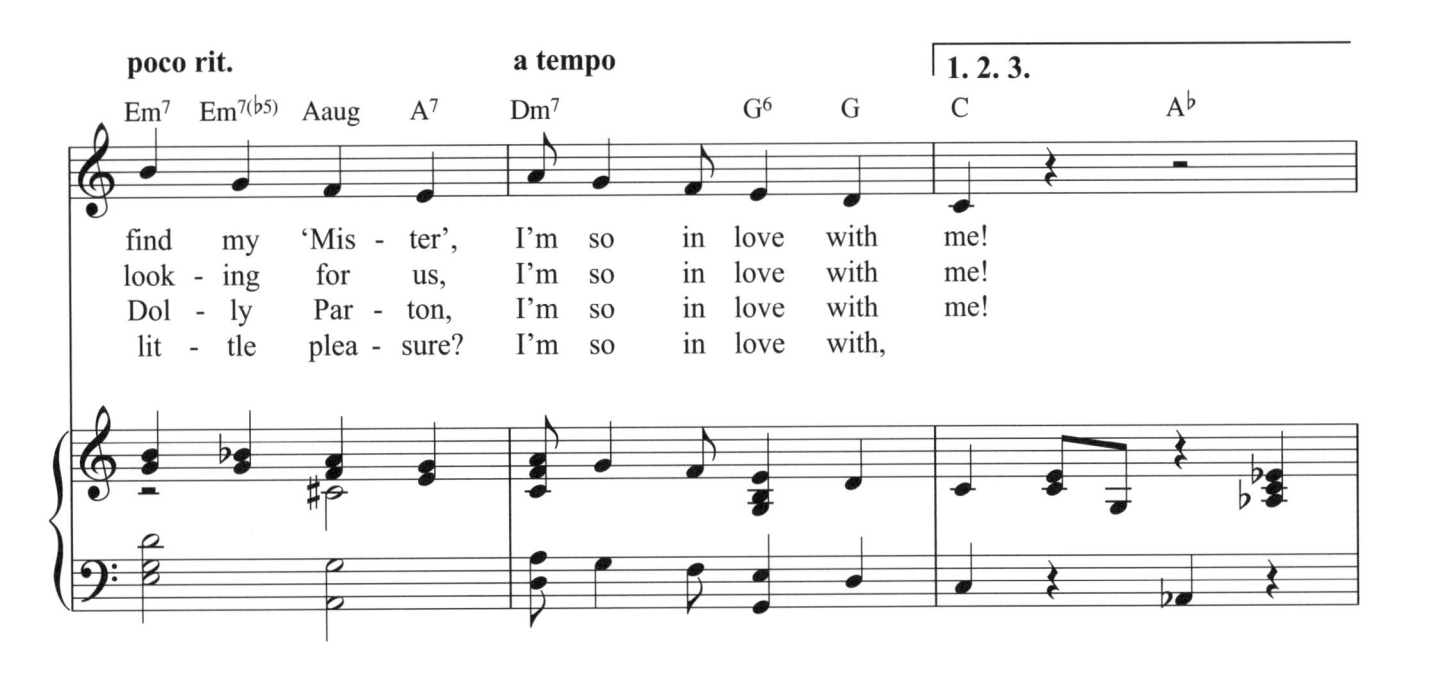

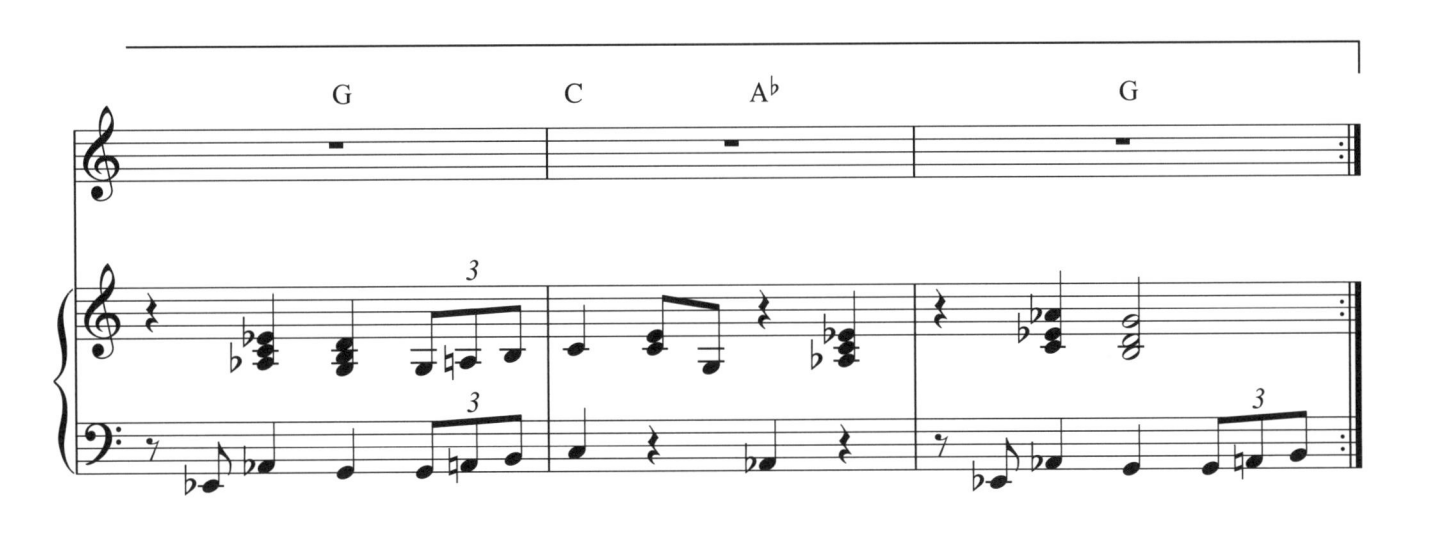

poco rit.   **a tempo**   **1. 2. 3.**

Em⁷   Em⁷⁽♭⁵⁾   Aaug   A⁷   Dm⁷   G⁶   G   C   A♭

find my 'Mis - ter', I'm so in love with me!
look - ing for us, I'm so in love with me!
Dol - ly Par - ton, I'm so in love with me!
lit - tle plea - sure? I'm so in love with,

G   C   A♭   G

4.

Em⁷   Aaug   A   Dm⁷   G⁶   G⁷/D   C   G⁷   C

I'm so in love with, I'm so in love with me!   WITH ME!

41

YOU'RE GOING TO THE BALL

(Solo Fairy Godmother, Fairy Brigade and Chorus)

[Fairy G: Well of course, my dear. You don't think I'd waste my time and talents on any old event do you?!]

With rubato ♩ = c. 60

Fairy Godmother

1. Don't you wor-ry Cin-de-rel-la, I have come to make things bet-ter!
2. Let me tell you Cin-de-rel-la, I'll find you the per-fect fel-la!
3. Lis-ten to me Cin-de-rel-la, there's one thing you must re-mem-ber,

To Coda

Leave your chores and dir-ty dish-es, I am here to grant your wish-es!
Just when you thought life was o-ver, hel-lo li-mo! Good-bye so-fa!
all my spells will lose their pow-er when you hear that mid-night hour.

Words and Music by Mark and Helen Johnson
© 2008 Out of the Ark Ltd, Middlesex TW12 2HD
CCLI Song No. 5183883

a little faster
FGM and Fairy Brigade
E♭ F B♭maj7 Bdim7 E♭ F E♭/F F
Here's a touch of ma-gic just to help us on our way, sprin-kled with a flou-rish and a
Here's a touch of ma-gic just to help us on our way, sprin-kled with a flou-rish and a
B♭maj7 D7 Gm7 D7 Gm7
twirl! Spread a lit-tle star-dust, find some spe-cial words to say, and
twirl! Spread a lit-tle star-dust, find some spe-cial words to say, and
rit.
Faster, with a swing ♩ = 128
Cm7 Fsus4 F B♭ B♭/D
soon we'll have a ve-ry dif-ferent girl!
soon we'll have a ve-ry dif-ferent girl!
You're go-ing to the

E♭ E♭/F F B♭maj7
ball! You're going to see it all!
Fdim7/G E♭/G Gm/F Cm Dm E♭ F7sus4 E♭/F
You're going to have the time of your life this
B♭sus4 Cm9 Dm7 E♭
eve - ning! You're in for a sur - prise,
E♭/F F B♭maj7 Fdim7/G E♭/G Gm/F
they won't be - lieve their eyes, but let me tell you
3

slower
Cm Dm E♭ F7sus4 F6 B♭2 B♭maj7 F11 E♭/F
now that you won't be dream - ing!
1.
B♭maj7 F11
2.
B♭maj7 F11 D.𝄋 al Coda
CODA
With a swing (♫ = ♩ ♪) ♩ = 128
F B♭ B♭/D E♭ E♭/F F
FGM and Fairy Brigade
You look so beau-ti-ful!
Fairy Brigade
You're go-ing to the ball! You're going to see it

B♭maj7 Fdim7/G E♭/G Gm/F Cm Dm E♭
You're just in - cre-di-ble! The mir - ror
all! You're going to have the time of your
F7sus4 E♭/F B♭sus4 Cm9 Dm7
on the wall says you're the best!
life this eve - ning! You're in for a sur-
3
E♭ E♭/F F B♭maj7
You look so beau-ti-ful! You're just in -
-prise, they won't be-lieve their eyes,
3

1.
Fdim7/G E♭/G Gm/F Cm Dm E♭ F7sus4 F6 B♭2 B♭
-cre-di-ble!
but let me tell you now that_ you won't be dream-ing!_
2. Fairy Godmother
B♭7 Cm Dm E♭ F7sus4 F6
The mir-ror on the wall won't
You're go-ing to the now that_ you won't be
molto rit.
B♭maj7 Cm7 Dm7 E♭maj7 F7 Gm7 Adim7 B♭13
lie.
dream-ing!

THERE'S A PARTY HERE TONIGHT

(All)

[Town Crier: Hear ye! Hear ye! It's time to partee!]

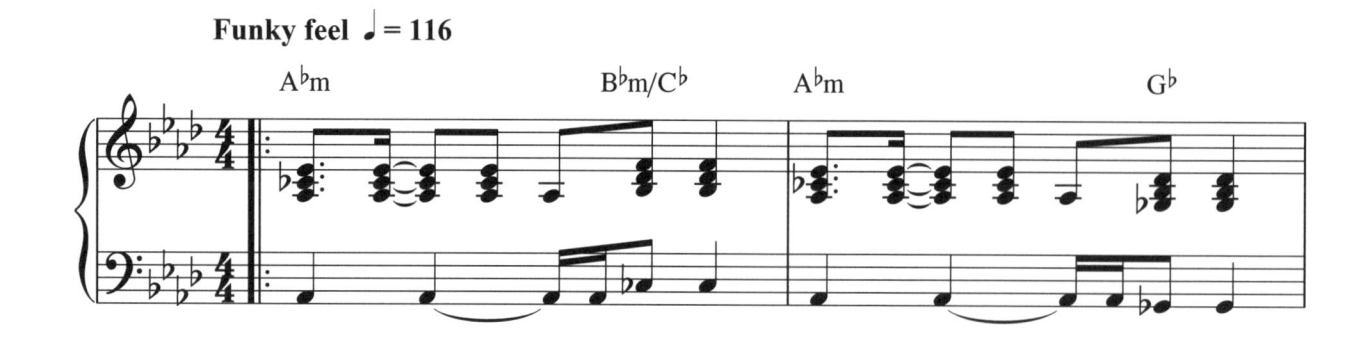

Funky feel ♩ = 116

1. Come on and

(2. 3. 4.) join the par - ty while the night is young! We've got the

Words and Music by Mark and Helen Johnson
© 2008 Out of the Ark Ltd, Middlesex TW12 2HD
CCLI Song No. 5183890

48

music started and we'll sing a-long! Go get your dancing shoes, put your glad rags on, there's a par-ty here to-night!

2. Come on and

2. 3. 4.
A♭5
C♭ A♭/C (clap)
Clap your hands!
D♭ B♭/D
Tap your feet!
E♭ Fm7
Swing your hips to the
B♭m E♭
rhy - thm.
C♭ A♭/C
Move your head
D♭ B♭/D
to the beat,
E♭ Fm7
use the groove you've been

D.𝄋 al Coda on 4º
B♭m7 A♭/B♭ B♭m7 D♭/E♭ E♭
giv - - en! 3. Come on and
CODA
A♭ B♭m7 E♭7sus4 E♭m9
there's a par - ty here to - night!
A♭ B♭m7 E♭7sus4 E♭m9
there's a par - ty here to - night!
A♭ B♭m7 E♭ A♭5

A TON OF LOVE

(Baker(s), Ugly Sisters and Chorus)

[M. Bunn: Ladies please! We need to get started. I'm going to need plenty of help with this. A wedding cake is a tricky thing to get right.]

With a swing ($\sqrt{}\sqrt{} = \sqrt{}^3\sqrt{}$) ♩ = 132

Bakers, Ugly Sisters and Chorus

1. If he wants a wed-ding (4.) cake,
   (2.) laughs
   (3.) ears

that's ex-act-ly what we'll make. It may take
and a sop-py pho-to-graph. Add com-mon
and a tis-sue for your tears, three spoons of

Words and Music by Mark and Helen Johnson
© 2008 Out of the Ark Ltd, Middlesex TW12 2HD
CCLI Song No. 5183900

time, but it's just fine, that's what it takes!
sense, try com-pli-ments and you'll go far!
grace im-proves the taste for ma-ny years.

It's a com-pli-ca-ted list, lots of things you must-n't
Take a health-y dose of trust (and a pinch of fair-y
Take a buc-ket load of hugs, you can nev-er have e-

To Coda

miss. This re-ci-pe will gua-ran-tee just a lit-tle lift!
dust). There's one more thing you must put in, it's a ton of love!
-nough. There's one more thing you must put in, it's a ton of love!

Weigh it, sift it, check it's fresh, before you put it in, use the best ingredients and grease the baking tin!

1. 2. Take a tablespoon of tin! 4. If he wants a wedding
3. Take a pair of listening

D.S. al Coda

CODA

-tee just a little lift!

IF I HAD ONE WISH

(Cinderella and Rockerfella)

[Rocky: Oh Betta! Where could you be? I had you there and then I let you go. I wonder if we'll ever be together again!]

Thoughtfully ♩ = c. 108

Cinderella

1. In fair-y-tales and in pic-ture books there's a love that has to be won. The
(2.) charm-ing prince goes and falls in love with the spe-cial girl of his dreams. If

1. *Rockerfella*

dra-gon's slayed and a girl is saved, and a hap-pi-er life be-gun. 2. A
I could find who the slip-per fits, I would ask her to mar-ry

Words and Music by Mark and Helen Johnson
© 2008 Out of the Ark Ltd, Middlesex TW12 2HD
CCLI Song No. 5183917

2.
Both
Ab/Eb Eb Cb Db/Cb Ebm/Cb Db/Cb Cb Db/Cb
me. Ev - ery-thing was oh so per - fect, all the world was
Bb7sus4 Bb7 Rockerfella Gdim7 Abm Fdim7 Gb
mine! She was there in my arms and she smiled as we danced, and the
Cm7(b5) Dbsus4 Db Cinderella Gdim7 Abm
earth stood still in time. He was all I could see, we were
Fdim7 Gb Cm7(b5) Bbsus4 Bb Both Eb Eb2/Db
lost in a dream till I heard the mid-night chime. Now here I am on my

own a-gain, wish-ing you could be here to-night.

To Coda

Cinderella
If I had one wish, I'd wish my dreams came true. If I had one

1. **Rockerfella** **2.** *D.S. al Coda*
dream, my on-ly dream would be of you. If I you.

CODA

Cinders:
1. In fair-y-tales and in pic-ture books there's a love that has to be won. The dra-gon's slayed and a girl is saved, and a hap-pi-er life be-gun. If I

Rocky:
If I had one wish, I'd dream my dreams came true, if I had one dream, my on-ly dream would be of you. 2. A

charm-ing prince goes and falls in love with the spe-cial girl of his
had one wish, I'd dream my
dreams. If I could find who the slip-per fits, I would
dreams came true, if I had one dream, my on-ly
ask her to mar-ry me! Ev-ery-thing was
dream would be of you. Ev-ery-thing was

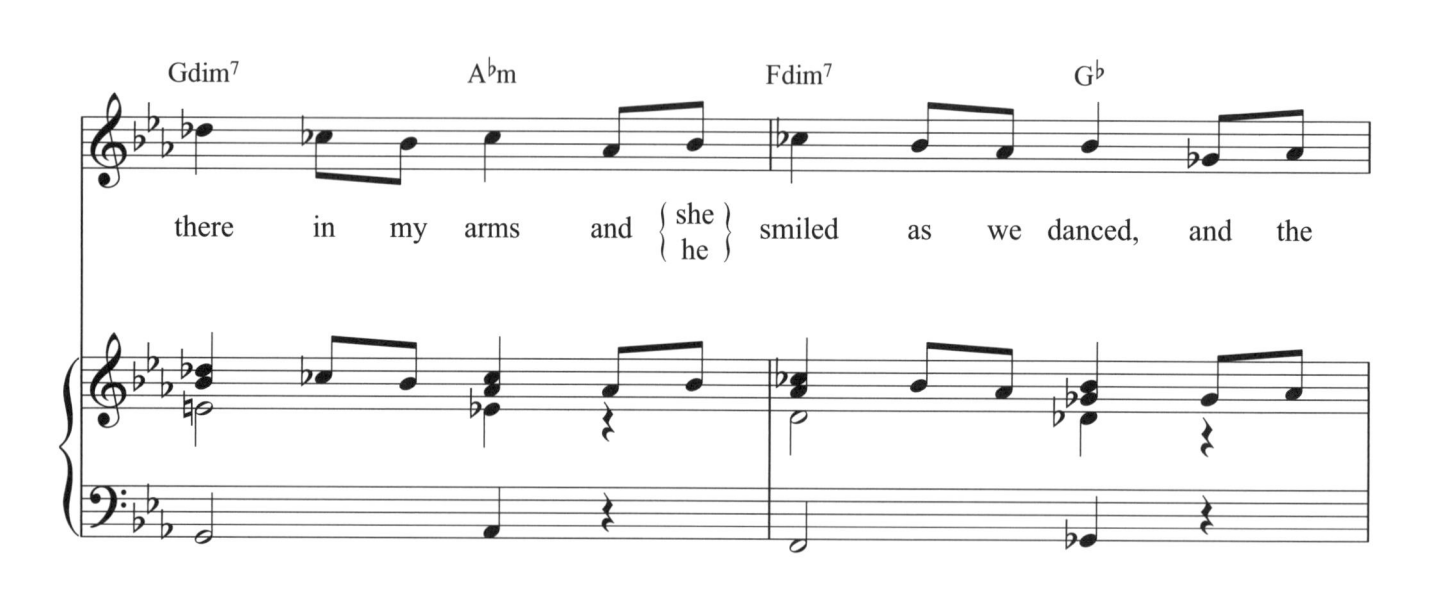

Both

oh so per-fect, all the world was mine! { She / He } was there in my arms and { she / he } smiled as we danced, and the earth stood still in time. { She / He } was all I could see, we were lost in a dream till I heard the mid-night chime. Now here I am on my own a-gain, wish-ing you could be here to-night.

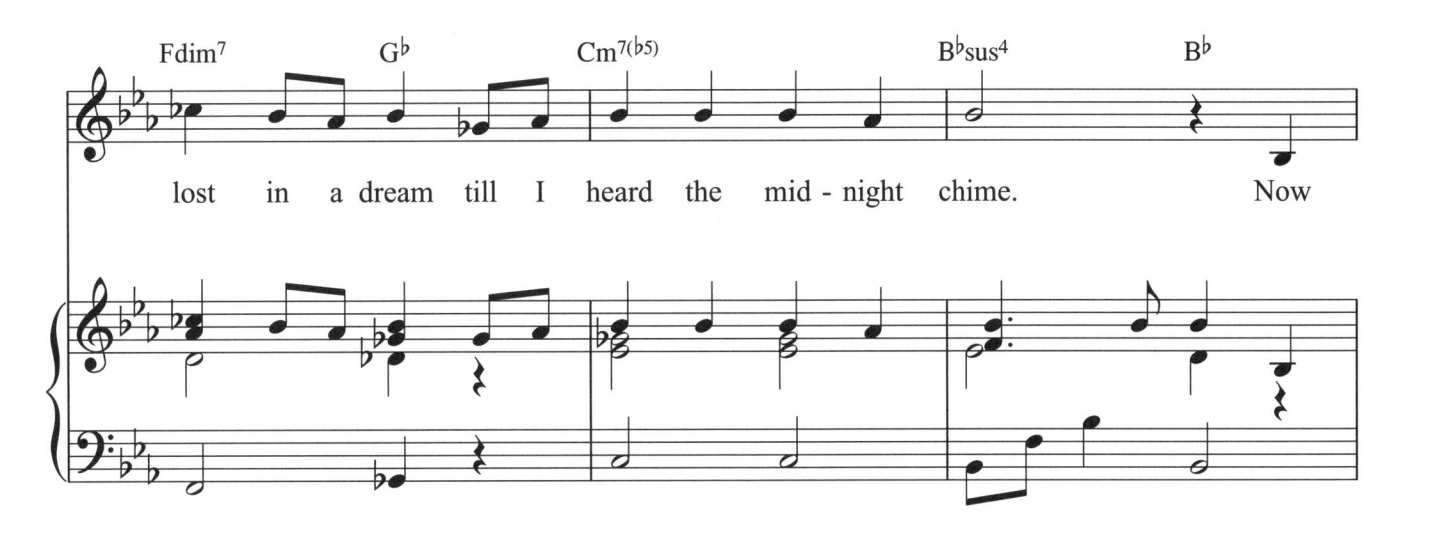

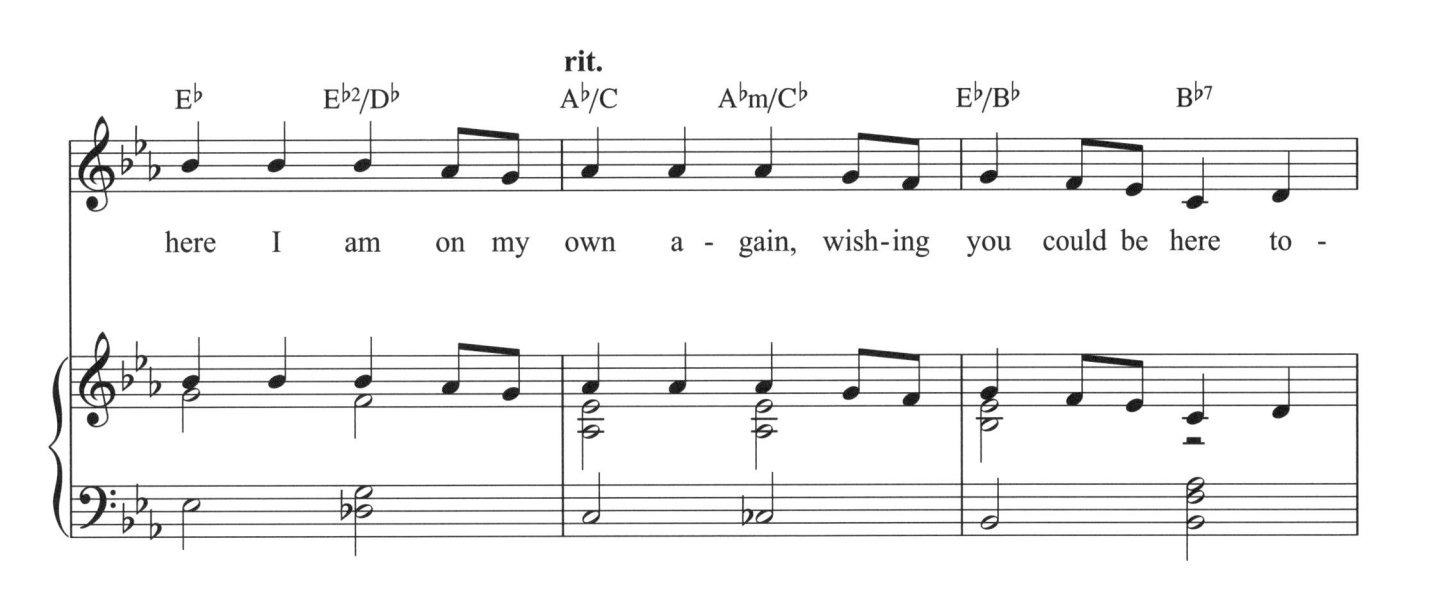

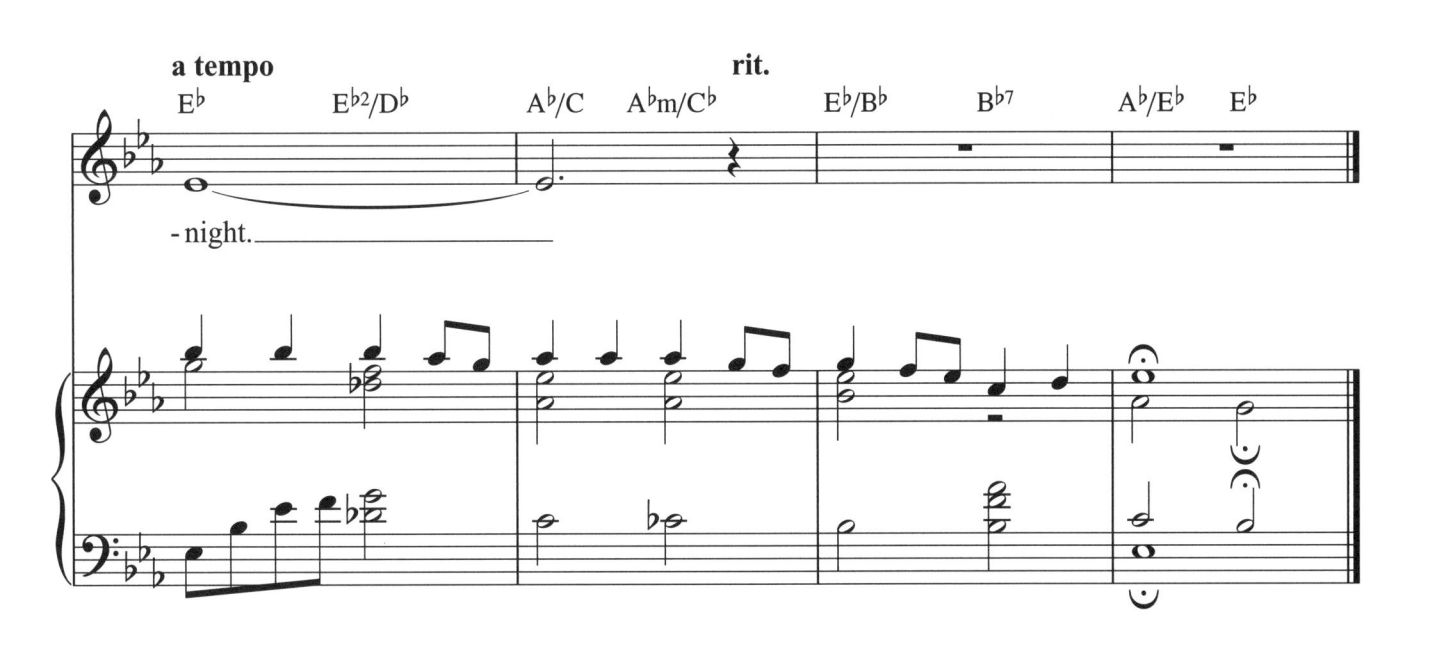

YOUR FEET ARE TOO BIG!

(All and audience)

[Footman: I don't think this is going to work, Madame. It's like trying to squeeze an elephant into a tube of Smarties!]

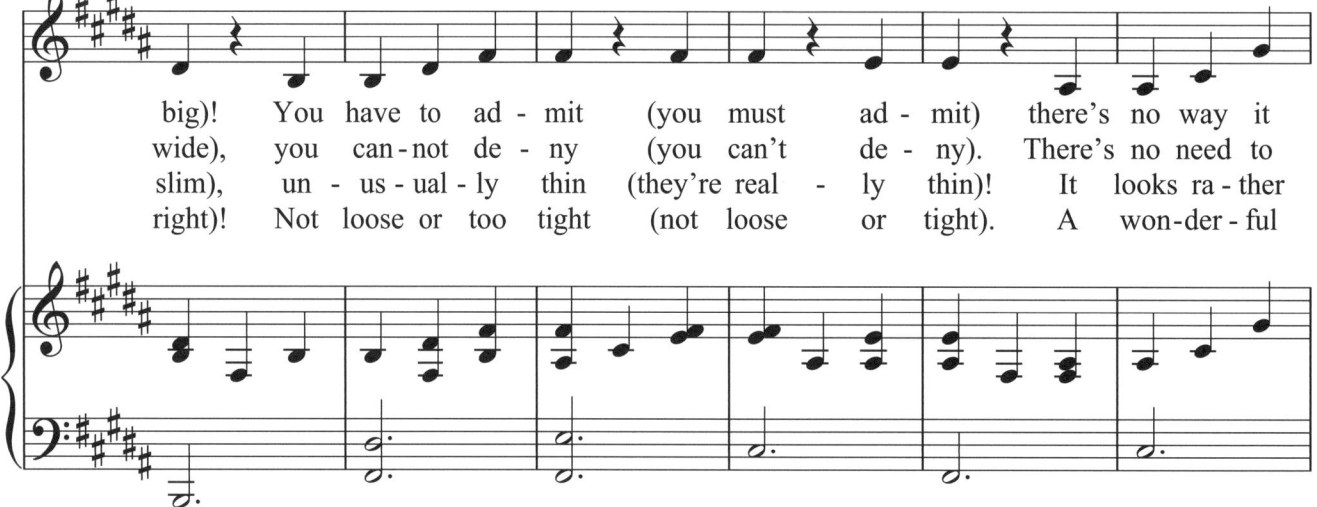

Steadily ♩= 174

1. Your feet are too big (too big, too big)! You have to ad-mit (you must ad-mit) there's no way it
(2.) feet are too wide (too wide, too wide), you can-not de-ny (you can't de-ny). There's no need to
(3.) feet are too slim (too slim, too slim), un-u-sual-ly thin (they're real-ly thin)! It looks ra-ther
(4.) *Instrumental* (with dialogue – see block text)
(5.) feet are just right (just right, just right)! Not loose or too tight (not loose or tight). A won-der-ful

Words by Mark and Helen Johnson
Music by Johann Strauss II, adapted by Mark and Helen Johnson
© 2008 Out of the Ark Ltd, Middlesex TW12 2HD
CCLI Song No. 5183924

fits (no way it fits), you're o-ver e-quipped (o-ver e-quipped)!
cry (no need to cry), they don't fit in-side (don't fit in-side)!
grim (so grim, so grim), you'd get them both in (get them both in)!
sight (won-der-ful sight)! Well, there's a sur-prise (sur-prise, sur-prise)!

I'm sor-ry to say (sor-ry to say), please be on your way (be on your way). I know it's a shame, all the
I'm sor-ry to say (sor-ry to say), please be on your way (be on your way). I know it's a shame, all the
I'm sor-ry to say (sor-ry to say), please be on your way (be on your way). I know it's a shame, all the
I'm hap-py to say (hap-py to say), it's turned out O-K (turned out O-K). It's been a good day, hip hoo-

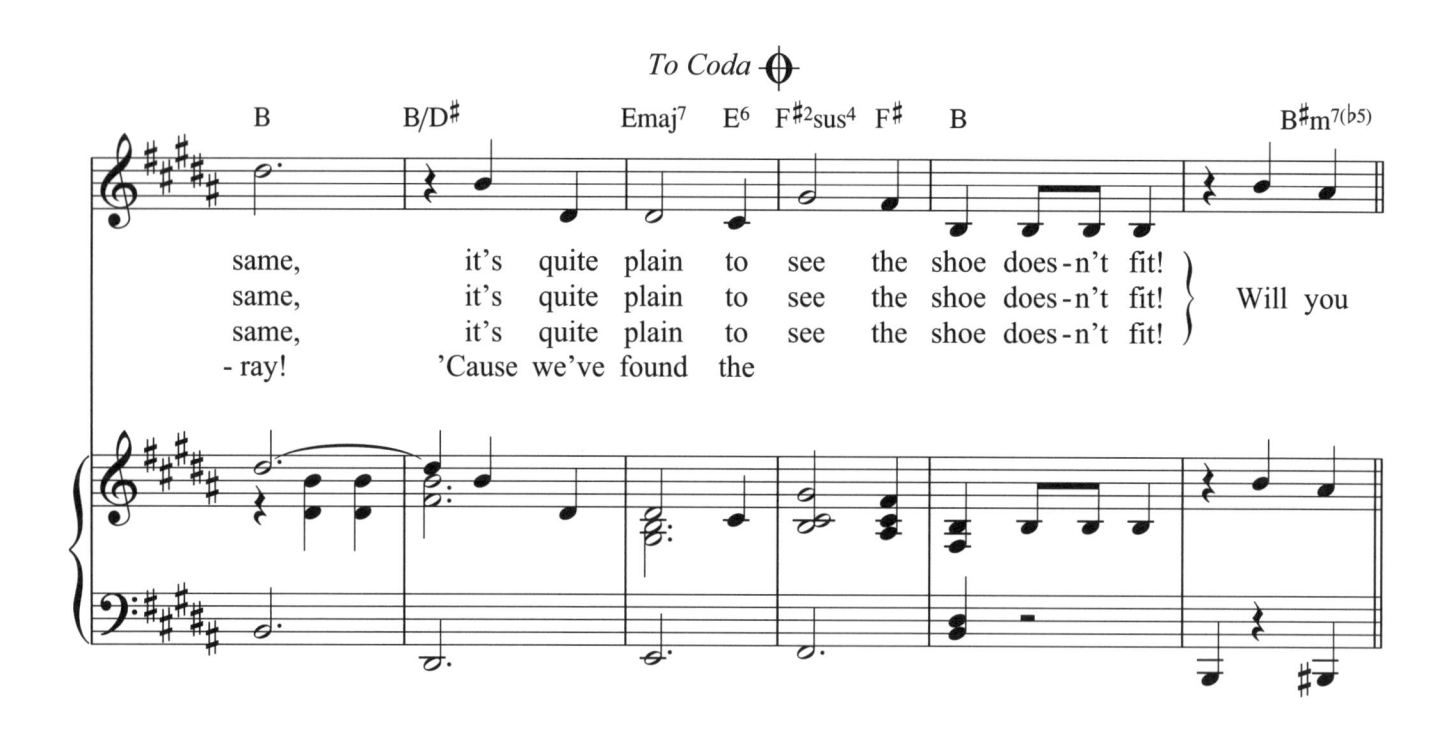

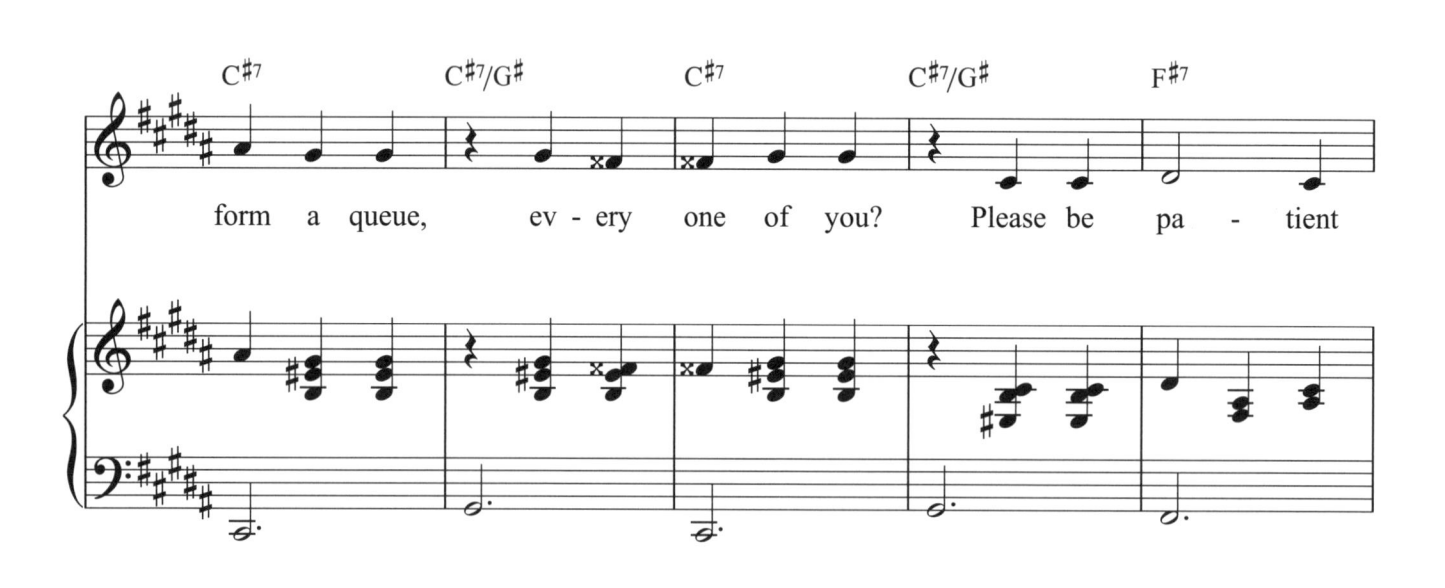

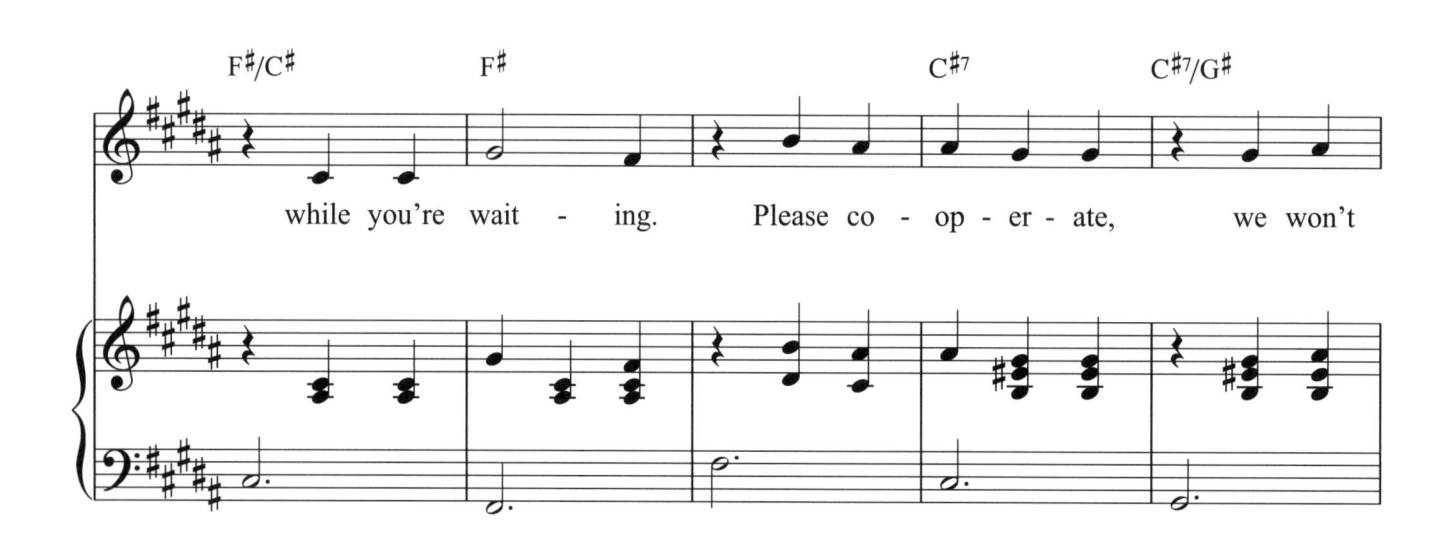

same, it's quite plain to see the shoe does-n't fit!
same, it's quite plain to see the shoe does-n't fit! } Will you
same, it's quite plain to see the shoe does-n't fit!
-ray! 'Cause we've found the

form a queue, ev-ery one of you? Please be pa-tient

while you're wait-ing. Please co-op-er-ate, we won't

Lyrics (sung):
keep you late, there's just half a chance you'll be the lucky one to-day!

{ 2. Your
  3. Your
  4. *Instrumental* (see block text) }

5. Your

CODA

girl the shoe's gon-na fit!

4   INSTRUMENTAL VERSE (with dialogue:)

Rocky   (Calling out) Is there anyone else?
Town Crier   (Calling even louder) Anyone else?
Ugly S (Tog)   Oh no there isn't! Let me try again. (Both try to get back to the chair)
Rocky   Looks like that's it then, everyone.
PR   Never mind Rocky there's plenty more feet in the street. Go on tour and check out all the feet abroad.
Ugly S (Tog)   I've got broad feet!

Buttons and Cinders run on.

Buttons   Wait! There's one more! Cinderella! (She tries on shoe)
Rocky   It fits! There, that's Betta!

HAPPY EVER AFTERS

(All)

[Buttons: An offstage inspector one day
Happened to come to our play.
When his verdict he gave,
He did nothing but rave,
And the fairies all went...

Fairy Brg: Wey hey, hey!]

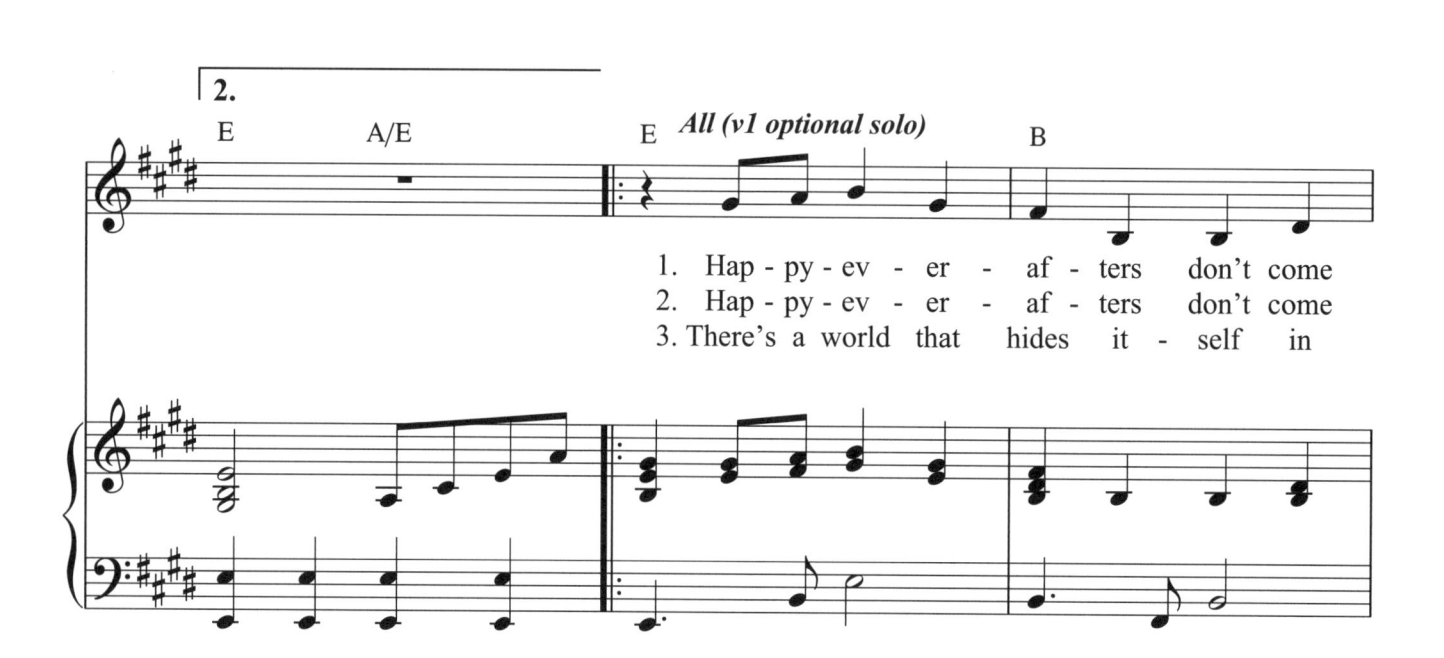

With energy ♩ = 150

All (v1 optional solo)

1. Hap - py - ev - er - af - ters   don't come
2. Hap - py - ev - er - af - ters   don't come
3. There's a world that hides it - self in

Words and Music by Mark and Helen Johnson
© 2008 Out of the Ark Ltd, Middlesex TW12 2HD
CCLI Song No. 5183931

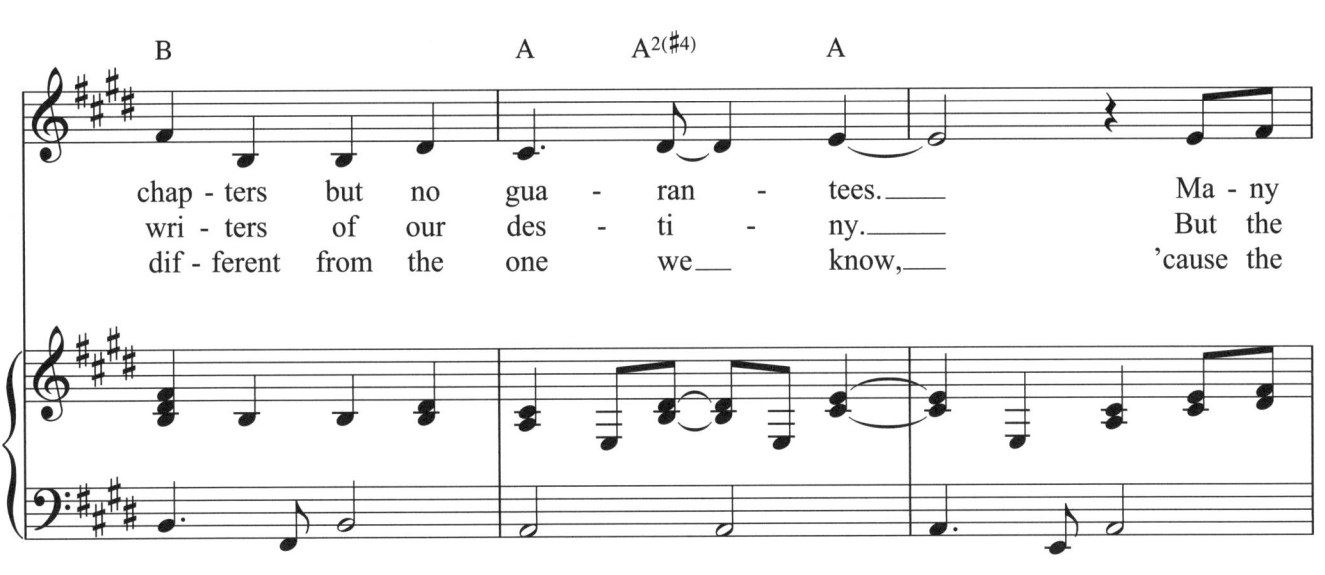

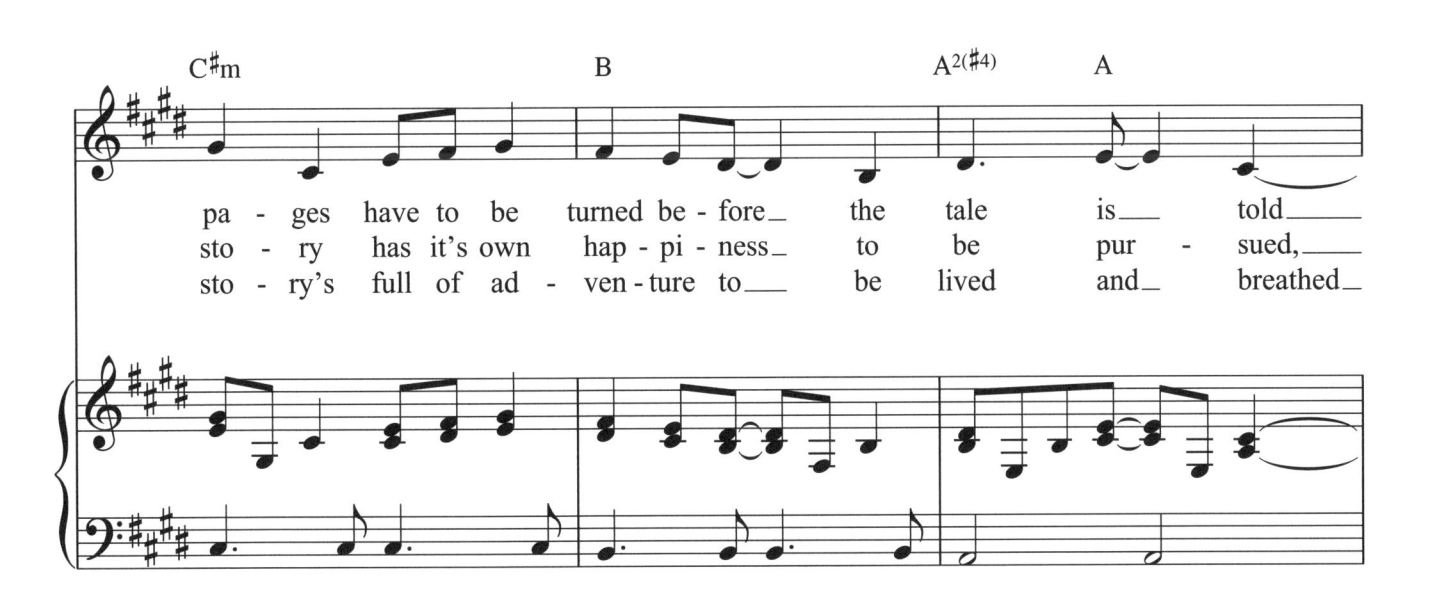

ea - si - ly,___ there are ma - ny
ea - si - ly,___ none of us are
fair - y tales___ and it's not so

chap - ters but no guar - an - tees.___ Ma - ny
wri - ters of our des - ti - ny.___ But the
dif - ferent from the one we___ know,___ 'cause the

pa - ges have to be turned be - fore___ the tale is___ told___
sto - ry has it's own hap - pi - ness___ to be pur - sued,___
sto - ry's full of ad - ven - ture to___ be lived and___ breathed___

68

69

(2º only)
Esus4 E
A/E E
Dsus4 D
G/D D
Part 1
-rel - la!
Roc-ker - fel - la!
Part 2
Hap - - py ev - er af - -
D2 D
A A2 A
Asus4 A
Got to - ge - ther.
Cin - de -
- ter, our sto - ry
E2 E
E2 E
E2 E
A/B
- rel - la and her fel - la got to - ge - ther.
Cin - de -
ends.

Esus4 E A/E E Dsus4 D G/D D
-rel - la! Roc-ker - fel - la!
Hap - - - py ev - er af - - -
D2 D A A2 A Asus4 A
Got to - ge - ther. Cin - de -
-ter, our sto - ry
D E D E D E
1.
D E A/E
-rel - la and her fel - la got to -
(Part 1 start) Cin - de -
comes to a ve - ry hap - py end!

-ge - ther. Hap — py ev - er
-py end! Hap — py ev - er
af — ter, our sto — ry
comes to a ve - ry hap - py end!

TONIGHT'S THE NIGHT

Prog Seller: Get your souvenir programme here! Free cut out Rocky doll with seven outfits! Sell on ebay next week for a huge profit!

ALL
1. Tonight's the night!
   At last the moment's arrived.
   You don't want to miss it!
   The buzz! The hype!
   The streets are coming alive,
   So come buy your tickets!

   CHORUS   *Rockerfella! Rockerfella!*
   Head-to-toe designer leather,
   Come and see the hottest thing around!
   Rockerfella! Rockerfella!
   One night only, now or never,
   Come and get your tickets to the greatest show in town!

2. Tonight's the night!
   The curtain's ready to rise.
   You don't want to miss it!
   The sound, the lights
   Are guaranteed to delight,
   So come buy your tickets!

   CHORUS

3. Tonight's the night!
   We're gonna head for the heights.
   You don't want to miss it!
   The smells! The sights!
   The songs to thrill and excite,
   So come buy your tickets!

   CHORUS   *Rockerfella! Rockerfella!*
   Head-to-toe designer leather,
   Come and see the hottest thing around!
   Rockerfella! Rockerfella!
   One night only, now or never,
   Come and get your tickets to the greatest show,
   Come and get your tickets to the greatest show,
   Come and get your tickets to the greatest show in town!

Words and Music by Mark and Helen Johnson
© 2008 Out of the Ark Ltd, Middlesex TW12 2HD
CCLI Song No. 5183845

A FRIEND LIKE YOU

Cinders: Oh I know a better song than that!

CHORUS
CINDERELLA
I'm glad to have a friend like you,
Buttons I know it's true, you're there for me.
BUTTONS
I'm here and we're a funny pair,
Cinders you know I care about you.

BUTTONS
1   I remember when you first became my friend,
We'd dream of who we'd like to be.
Many were the days we played our games of make-believe.
CINDERELLA
You would be the cowboy racing down the railroad,
Off to set a poor girl free!
BOTH
We'd ride off together in the sunset, you and me!

CHORUS

CINDERELLA
2   You're the dashing prince, got turned into a frog —
An evil act of sorcery.
BUTTONS
You're the lucky girl who plants a kiss upon my cheek!
CINDERELLA
I would be the princess locked up in a castle,
Nobody to rescue me.
BUTTONS
I would be your knight in shining armour, you'd go free!

CHORUS x 2 *(both sing second time)*

Cinders/Buttons you know, I care about you.

Words and Music by Mark and Helen Johnson
© 2008 Out of the Ark Ltd, Middlesex TW12 2HD
CCLI Song No. 5183852

IT'S NOT ALL IT'S CRACKED UP TO BE

Dan Deeny: Oh come on now Rocky – don't throw it all away! I don't want to be the one who's gonna have to beg you to stay...

CHORUS

ROCKERFELLA
Oh, it's not all it's cracked up to be!
I've lived a life of fame and celebrity.
I've had my name in lights, done concerts every night,
And it's not all it's cracked up to be!

PAPARAZZI
Oh, it's not all it's cracked up to be!
He's lived a life of fame and celebrity.
He's had his name in lights, done concerts every night,
And it's not all it's cracked up to be!

ROCKERFELLA
1 I've headlined every continent, I've toured around the world,
   From Sydney to New York and back again.
   I've had my share of compliments from screaming crowds of girls,
   But stardom isn't everything they'd say.

CHORUS *(Paparazzi)*

DAN DEENY
2 I took you from obscurity, I made you what you are.
   It's thanks to me that you're a household name.
   I've given you security, the chauffeur and the car.
   I can't believe you'd throw it all away!

CHORUS *(Paparazzi)*

DAN DEENY CHORUS
I can't believe you'd throw it all away!
Maybe you need to take a holiday.
You're just a little stressed, so get yourself a rest.
Come to your senses and we'll talk again!

CHORUS *(Paparazzi)*

ROCKERFELLA
3 The lifestyle of a megastar has lost its gloss for me.
   I'm ready to discard my dancing shoes.
DAN DEENY
   If you give up on your guitar you have my guarantee,
   Within a week I'll find somebody new!

CHORUS and DAN DEENY CHORUS together, followed by CHORUS

Words and Music by Mark and Helen Johnson
© 2008 Out of the Ark Ltd, Middlesex TW12 2HD
CCLI Song No. 5183869

I'M SO IN LOVE WITH ME!

Anastacia: Only because you're always picking your nose! Carl says I've got skin like a baby.
Augustina: Yes dear, a baby rhinoceros!

1.   ANAS   How could anybody think we're sisters?
    AUG   It's a total mystery to me!
    ANAS   My dainty feet!
    AUG   My rosy cheeks!
    BOTH   How could any poor old man resist us?!
    ANAS   Maybe I should try a brighter lipstick?
    AUG   Maybe add a tub of wrinkle cream.
    BOTH   I'm on a quest to find my 'Mister',
              I'm so in love with me!

2.   AUG   Would you say my bottom looks enormous?
              Should I try a brighter shade of green?
              I can't decide.
    ANAS   Take my advice,
              Close your eyes and say "I'm looking gorgeous!"
    AUG   Blow a kiss in front of all the cameras,
    ANAS   We'll be everything they want to see!
    BOTH   Fellas will all be looking for us,
              I'm so in love with me!

3.   ANAS   Sing a song of 'Happy Ever After',
    AUG   Sing a song of 'Will You Marry Me?'
    ANAS   Whisked off my feet,
    AUG   Held cheek to cheek,
    BOTH   Honeymoon in sunny Costa Brava!
    ANAS   See me rubbing shoulders with the film stars,
    AUG   See my face in 'Hello' magazine.
    BOTH   Time to move over Dolly Parton,
              I'm so in love with me!

4.   AUG   One day I'll be Mrs Rockerfella,
    ANAS   One day you'll be married – in your dreams!
    AUG   I'll be the bride.
    ANAS   I'd be surprised!
    BOTH   Hand-in-hand we'll walk the aisle together.
    AUG   Think of Fred Astaire and Ginger Rogers,
    ANAS   More like Tweedledum and Tweedledee!
    BOTH   Don't I deserve a little pleasure?
              I'm so in love with, I'm so in love with,
              I'm so in love with me!
              WITH ME!

Words and Music by Mark and Helen Johnson
© 2008 Out of the Ark Ltd, Middlesex TW12 2HD
CCLI Song No. 5183876

YOU'RE GOING TO THE BALL

Fairy G: Well of course, my dear. You don't think I'd waste my time and talents on any old event do you?!

FAIRY GODMOTHER
1   Don't you worry Cinderella,
    I have come to make things better!
    Leave your chores and dirty dishes,
    I am here to grant your wishes!

FAIRY G and FAIRY BRIGADE
Here's a touch of magic just to help us on our way,
Sprinkled with a flourish and a twirl!
Spread a little stardust, find some special words to say,
And soon we'll have a very different girl!

Sing echo on last chorus only

CHORUS   *You're going to the ball!*   (You look so beautiful)
         You're going to see it all!   (You're just incredible)
         You're going to have the time of your life, this evening!
                                (The mirror on the wall says you're the best!)
         You're in for a surprise,   (You look so beautiful)
         They won't believe their eyes, (You're just incredible)
         But let me tell you now that you won't be dreaming!

FAIRY GODMOTHER
2   Let me tell you Cinderella,
    I'll find you the perfect fella!
    Just when you thought life was over,
    Hello limo! Goodbye sofa!

FAIRY G and FAIRY BRIGADE (Here's a touch of magic ...)

CHORUS

FAIRY GODMOTHER
3   Listen to me Cinderella,
    There's one thing you must remember,
    All my spells will lose their power
    When you hear that midnight hour.

CHORUS x 2 *(with echo)*

LAST LINE   *But let me tell you now that you won't be dreaming!*
                                (The mirror on the wall won't lie)

Words and Music by Mark and Helen Johnson
© 2008 Out of the Ark Ltd, Middlesex TW12 2HD
CCLI Song No. 5183883

THERE'S A PARTY HERE TONIGHT

Town Crier: Hear ye! Hear ye! It's time to partee!

    ALL
1. Come on and join the party while the night is young!
   We've got the music started and we'll sing along!
   Go get your dancing shoes,
   Put your glad rags on,
   There's a party here tonight!
   (Repeat)

                                                                                     Add claps and actions:

    CHORUS   *Clap your hands!*   *(clap, clap)*
                        Tap your feet!   *(tap, tap – with feet!)*
                        Swing your hips to the rhythm.   *(swing hips along with vocal)*
                        Move your head   *(tilt head left then right)*
                        To the beat,   *(click fingers, or action of choice)*
                        Use the groove you've been given!

2. Come on and join the party while the night is young!
   We've got the music started and we'll sing along!
   Go get your dancing shoes,
   Put your glad rags on,
   There's a party here tonight!

    CHORUS

3. Come on and join the party while the night is young!
   We've got the music started and we'll sing along!
   Go get your dancing shoes,
   Put your glad rags on,
   There's a party here tonight!
   There's a party here tonight!
   There's a party here tonight!

Words and Music by Mark and Helen Johnson
© 2008 Out of the Ark Ltd, Middlesex TW12 2HD
CCLI Song No. 5183890

A TON OF LOVE

M. Bunn: Ladies please! We need to get started. I'm going to need plenty of help with this. A wedding cake is a tricky thing to get right.

       BAKER(S), UGLY SISTERS & CHORUS

1. If he wants a wedding cake,
That's exactly what we'll make.
It may take time but it's just fine,
That's what it takes!
It's a complicated list,
Lots of things you mustn't miss.
This recipe will guarantee
Just a little lift!

    CHORUS   *Weigh it, sift it, check it's fresh before you put it in,
Use the best ingredients and grease the baking tin!*

2. Take a tablespoon of laughs
And a soppy photograph.
Add common sense, try compliments
And you'll go far!
Take a healthy dose of trust
(And a pinch of fairy dust).
There's one more thing you must put in,
It's a ton of love!

    CHORUS

3. Take a pair of listening ears
And a tissue for your tears,
Three spoons of grace improves the taste
For many years.
Take a bucket load of hugs,
You can never have enough.
There's one more thing you must put in,
It's a ton of love!

    CHORUS

4. *Repeat verse 1*

Words and Music by Mark and Helen Johnson
© 2008 Out of the Ark Ltd, Middlesex TW12 2HD
CCLI Song No. 5183900

IF I HAD ONE WISH

Rocky: Oh Betta! Where could you be? I had you there and then I let you go. I wonder if we'll ever be together again!

CINDERELLA

1. In fairytales and picture books
   There's a love that has to be won.
   The dragon's slayed and a girl is saved,
   And a happier life begun.

ROCKERFELLA

2. A charming prince goes and falls in love
   With the special girl of his dreams.
   If I could find who the slipper fits,
   I would ask her to marry me!

CHORUS

BOTH
Everything was oh so perfect,
All the world was mine!
ROCKERFELLA
She was there in my arms
And she smiled as we danced,
And the earth stood still in time.
CINDERELLA
He was all I could see,
We were lost in a dream
Till I heard the midnight chime.
BOTH
Now here I am on my own again,
Wishing you could be here tonight.

BRIDGE

CINDERELLA
If I had one wish, I'd wish my dreams came true,
If I had one dream, my only dream would be of you.
(Repeat - ROCKERFELLA)

CHORUS

3. *Repeat verse 1 (CINDERELLA) and Bridge (ROCKERFELLA) together*

4. *Repeat verse 2 (ROCKERFELLA) and Bridge (CINDERELLA) together*

CHORUS *(BOTH)*

Words and Music by Mark and Helen Johnson
© 2008 Out of the Ark Ltd, Middlesex TW12 2HD
CCLI Song No. 5183917

YOUR FEET ARE TOO BIG!

Footman: I don't think this is going to work, Madame. It's like trying to squeeze an elephant into a tube of Smarties!

    ALL
1. Your feet are too big, (too big, too big)!
You have to admit (you must admit)
There's no way it fits (no way it fits),
You're over equipped (over equipped)!
I'm sorry to say (sorry to say),
Please be on your way (be on your way).
I know it's a shame, all the same,
It's quite plain to see the shoe doesn't fit!

    CHORUS   *Will you form a queue, every one of you?*
                       Please be patient while you're waiting.
                       Please co-operate, we won't keep you late,
                       There's just half a chance you'll be the lucky one today!

    ALL & AUDIENCE
2. Your feet are too wide (too wide, too wide),
You cannot deny (you can't deny).
There's no need to cry (no need to cry),
They don't fit inside (don't fit inside)!
I'm sorry to say (sorry to say),
Please be on your way (be on your way).
I know it's a shame, all the same,
It's quite plain to see the shoe doesn't fit!

    CHORUS

3. Your feet are too slim (too slim, too slim),
Unusually thin (they're <u>really</u> thin)!
It looks rather grim (so grim, so grim),
You'd get them both in (get them both in)!
I'm sorry to say (sorry to say),
Please be on your way (be on your way).
I know it's a shame, all the same,
It's quite plain to see the shoe doesn't fit!

    CHORUS

4. INSTRUMENTAL VERSE (with dialogue:)

    Rocky   *(Calling out)* Is there anyone else?

    Town Crier   *(Calling even louder)* Anyone else?

    Ugly S (Tog)   Oh no there isn't! Let me try again. *(Both try to get back to the chair)*

Rocky	Looks like that's it then, everyone.
PR	Never mind Rocky there's plenty more feet in the street. Go on tour and check out all the feet abroad.
Ugly S (Tog)	I've got broad feet!

Buttons and Cinders run on.

Buttons	Wait! There's one more! Cinderella! *(She tries on shoe)*
Rocky	It fits! There, that's Betta!

5 Your feet are just right (just right, just right)!
Not loose or too tight (not loose or tight).
A wonderful sight (wonderful sight)!
Well, there's a surprise (surprise, surprise)!
I'm happy to say (happy to say),
It's turned out OK (turned out OK).
It's been a good day, hip hooray!
'Cause we've found the girl the shoe's gonna fit!

Words by Mark and Helen Johnson
Music by Johann Strauss II, adapted by Mark and Helen Johnson
© 2008 Out of the Ark Ltd, Middlesex TW12 2HD
CCLI Song No. 5183924

HAPPY EVER AFTERS

Buttons: *An offstage inspector one day*
             Happened to come to our play.
             When his verdict he gave,
             He did nothing but rave,
             And the fairies all went...

Fairy Brg: *Wey hey, hey!*

OPTIONAL SOLO
1   Happy-ever-afters don't come easily,
    There are many chapters but no guarantees.
    Many pages have to be turned before the tale is told
    And the story takes you away from where you want to go.

                ALL
CHORUS (Part 1)
          Cinderella! Rockerfella!
          Got together.
          Cinderella and her fella got together.
          Cinderella! Rockerfella!
          Got together.
          Cinderella and her fella got together.

2   Happy-ever-afters don't come easily,
    None of us are writers of our destiny.
    But the story has its own happiness to be pursued,
    Every dream that somebody dares to follow can come true!

CHORUS (Part 1)

3   There's a world that hides itself in fairytales
    And it's not so different from the one we know,
    'Cause the story's full of adventure to be lived and breathed
    And I'm sure that anything's possible when you believe!

CHORUS (Part 1)

CHORUS (Part 2)
          Happy ever after, our story ends.
          Happy ever after, our story comes to a very happy end!

CHORUS (Parts 1 and 2 together)

          Happy ever after, our story comes to a very happy end!

Words and Music by Mark and Helen Johnson
© 2008 Out of the Ark Ltd, Middlesex TW12 2HD
CCLI Song No. 5183931

PERFORMANCE LICENCE APPLICATION FORM
(Cinderella & Rockerfella)

If you perform **Cinderella & Rockerfella** to an audience other than children and staff you will need a performance licence. If you have already purchased an instant performance licence then you do not need to do anything else. If you do not have a current performance licence then you can purchase one online at www.outoftheark.com. Alternatively you can photocopy and complete this form and return it by post or fax to Out of the Ark Music. If anticipated audience sizes are very small or if special circumstances apply please contact Out of the Ark Music.

The performance licence will permit the holder to:
- Perform **Cinderella & Rockerfella** during the licence period.
- Play the audio CD (either the backing or vocal tracks) at the performance(s).
- Reproduce the lyrics to the songs on printed paper, such as for programmes, and project the lyrics or display the lyrics electronically. The following credit should be included:
  'Reproduced by kind permission © Out of the Ark Ltd'.
- Photocopy the script for learning purposes. Copies must be destroyed after the performance.*
- Make no more than two copies of the music, to be used by participating musicians on the performance dates.*
- If you purchase a performance licence online you may also install your Words On Screen™ CD ROM onto your network server or onto two or more computers.

* UK state schools should report any copying of the lyrics and music on their Printed Music Licence (PML) returns.

If the performance is to be recorded please contact Out of the Ark Music.

We wish to apply for a licence to perform **Cinderella & Rockerfella** by Mark and Helen Johnson

Customer number (if known): ....

Name of school / organisation: ....

Name of organiser / producer: ....

Email address of organiser / producer: ....

Invoice address: ....

....

Post code: ....   Country: ....

Telephone number: ....

This licence to perform **Cinderella & Rockerfella** will last for 12 months from the date of application and cover any amount of performances within that period.

If applying retrospectively please enter date of first performance: ....

Price of licence: £30.00

Tick one of the three payment options below: (Invoices will be sent with all licences)

☐ Please bill my school/nursery at the above address (UK schools/nurseries only)

☐ I enclose a cheque (Pounds Sterling) for £30.00 payable to Out of the Ark Music

☐ Please charge £30.00 to the following card: (Visa [not Electron], MasterCard & Maestro accepted)

Card No ....

Start Date _ _ / _ _ (MM/YY)   Expiry Date _ _ / _ _ (MM/YY)   3 digit security code: _ _ _ (last 3 digits on signature strip)

Address: Out of the Ark Music
Kingsway Business Park, Oldfield Road
Hampton, Middlesex TW12 2HD UK

Phone: +44 (0)20 8481 7200   Fax: +44 (0)20 8941 5548   Email: info@outoftheark.com

The licence fees shown on this form are for 2021 and include VAT at 20%. Prices may be subject to revision.